Employment Guarantee Schemes

Employment Guarantee Schemes

Job Creation and Policy in Developing Countries and Emerging Markets

Edited by Michael J. Murray and Mathew Forstater

palgrave
macmillan

EMPLOYMENT GUARANTEE SCHEMES

First published in 2012 by
PALGRAVE MACMILLAN®
in the United States—a division of St. Martin's Press LLC,
175 Fifth Avenue, New York, NY 10010.

Where this book is distributed in the UK, Europe and the rest of the World, this is by Palgrave Macmillan, a division of Macmillan Publishers Limited, registered in England, company number 785998, of Houndmills, Basingstoke, Hampshire RG21 6XS.

Palgrave Macmillan is the global academic imprint of the above companies and has companies and representatives throughout the world.

ISBN: 978–1–137–32477–1

Library of Congress Cataloging-in-Publication Data

Employment guarantee schemes : job creation and policy in developing countries and emerging markets / edited by Michael J. Murray and Mathew Forstater.
pages cm
Includes bibliographical references.
ISBN 978–1–137–32477–1 (alk. paper)
1. Full employment policies—Developing countries. 2. Manpower policy—Developing countries. 3. Job creation—Developing countries. 4. Employment (Economic theory) 5. Unemployment—Developing countries. I. Murray, Michael J. II. Forstater, Mathew, 1961–
HD5852.E575 2013
331.12′0424091724—dc23 2012046507

A catalogue record of the book is available from the British Library.

Design by Integra Software Services

First edition: May 2013

10 9 8 7 6 5 4 3 2 1

Contents

List of Figures and Tables

Figures

Tables

Acknowledgments

The editors would like to thank Sara Dennison and Melissa Remick for their editorial assistance and their hard work in compiling the index.

Introduction: Employment Guarantee Schemes—Development, Environment, and Community

Michael J. Murray and Mathew Forstater

In the late 1990s, a number of economists and policymakers revived the idea of government-sponsored Job Guarantee (JG). Such a policy would assure a public service job for anyone who was ready and willing to work but could not find employment in the private sector or in the regular public sector. In the last two decades, there were a number of workshops, conferences, and special issues in academic journals, focusing on unemployment and strategies for full employment. During this initial stage, the focus was primarily on developing the theoretical basis of the JG approach to promoting full employment.

The current book is a part of a two-volume set on this topic. The first book—*The Job Guarantee: Toward True Full Employment* (Murray and Forstater, 2013)—emphasized theoretical developments, simulations, and applications for advanced industrialized economies. In contrast, this book, the second of the set, directs considerable attention to the challenges of and opportunities associated with enacting direct job creation policies in developing countries, including Ghana and Argentina, and BRICS (Brazil, Russia, India, China, and South Africa) economies. It is a collection of papers from both established and new scholars working on extending and elaborating various aspects of JG by means of formal modeling, simulations, case studies, and applications.

For developing and BRICS economies, the focus of the JG proposal shifts from the maintenance of effective demand to detailing how the

JG program promotes the construction of new infrastructure, the building of new capital, and the opening of new markets (Nell, et al. 2012). As such, the aim of this book is to investigate the importance of grassroots support for JG programs, and how JG might interface with other policy goals, such as environmental sustainability. Eschewing narrow individualistic and economistic approaches, the interdisciplinary, historical, and comparative studies discussed herein delve deeper into questions such as how both unemployment and true full employment can affect community.

The economic theory underlying JG is relatively simple, as Hyman P. Minsky (1986) outlined:

> The policy problem is to develop a strategy for full employment that does not lead to instability, inflation, and unemployment. The main instrument of such a policy is the creation of an infinitely elastic demand for labor at a floor or minimum wage that does not depend upon long- and short-run profit expectations of business. Since only government can divorce the offering of employment from the profitability of hiring workers, the infinitely elastic demand for labor must be created by government.
>
> (Minsky, 1986, p. 308)

The tenets underlying a JG program are that it (1) provides an infinitely elastic demand for labor, (2) hires off the bottom, (3) creates a pool of available and skilled laborers available for private-sector employment, (4) enhances human capital, and (5) generates valuable work (Tcherneva and Wray, 2005a, pp. 5–6). Some critics, however, claim that such a program would not be politically feasible and that it would be unaffordable; furthermore, they contend that it would not be possible to find workers to participate, and when work is done the jobs performed will not be useful. A potential reason for these critiques is that up to the present there has been very little empirical work on the JG approach.[1]

As discussed in this book, empirical analysis refutes many of these critiques. The JG program has been shown to be politically feasible in both developed and developing countries during times of economic crisis and structural change.

After the failed free market policies of the Hoover administration, a variant of the JG approach was enacted during the Great Depression era. The Roosevelt administration passed New Deal legislation that created the "alphabet agencies" from the Public Works Administration (PWA) to the Civilian Conservation Corp (CCC). The initiation of these programs came about with great fanfare. Not only were these programs politically feasible, but they provided examples of the useful work that public-sector employees can accomplish. For example, the PWA constructed the Oregon State Capital building and the Federal Trade Commission building in Washington, DC. In the case of the CCC, in a March 21, 1933, speech to Congress, President Roosevelt declared that the CCC's primary mission is to create:

> simple work . . . confining itself to forestry, the prevention of soil erosion, flood control, and similar projects. More important, however, than the material gains, will be the moral and spiritual value of such work.

The US experience shows that the JG design must engage people in work by creating socially useful projects while simultaneously enhancing human capital and worker morale. Perhaps the greatest initial accomplishment of the CCC program was that it mobilized 250,000 American youth in the first three months of its existence. This achievement was the biggest peacetime mobilization of workers in US history. The CCC program lasted until 1942, employed more than 3 million workers, and operated in all 50 US states. That most of the CCC projects constructed during this period are still in use is a testament to their functionality and worth.

In 1933, Roosevelt also established the Federal Emergency Relief Administration (FERA). Like the CCC, FERA had two goals that are important for contemporary JG proposals. The first goal was to counteract the belief that receiving work relief was shameful and the second was to restore the work ethic for over a quarter of the American population who had experienced long durations of unemployment.

Important to the restoration of work ethic is to distinguish the JG projects from "make work" to providing useful "work relief." The FERA programs included both blue-collar manual labor and white-collar professional work. In both instances, the work was "real work" (Rose, 1994, pp. 29–32), meaning that work was undertaken not for the sake of work itself; rather, workers in FERA programs provided socially necessary services while meeting the needs of the population. White-collar jobs included providing adult education, clerical work for government agencies, work in libraries and art museums, and nursing and elderly care (ibid, pp. 42–43).

The design of contemporary JG programs may be different from that of generations past as societal needs are different. For example, programs can be designed to become an important part of the Green Revolution, thereby providing jobs while addressing current ecological concerns (see Forstater, 2004; Godin, Chapter 1, and Li, Chapter 2, this volume).

Nancy Rose's (1994; Chapter 7, this volume) investigation of the New Deal era provides inspiration for the establishment of permanent JG programs for both developed and developing regions. Further, the New Deal era sheds light on the central importance of community backing and grassroots support for such initiatives (see also Forstater, 2004, Chapter 6).

The present volume provides many examples of embryonic JG programs from which researchers can learn. In addition to the US experience with instituting the JG, China instituted the *Ningxia Ecological Immigration Program* (see Chapter 2), Argentina the *Jefes y Jefas de Hogares* (see Chapter 3), India the *National Rural Employment Guarantee Act* (see Chapter 4), and Ghana the *National Youth Employment Programme* (see Chapter 5). These programs all lack some of the fundamental features of an ideal JG program. For example, all the aforementioned JG-type programs, including US New Deal programs, contained restrictions on eligibility, compensation, and program length. Nevertheless, each program shares commonalities with traditional JG proposals and is set up to address specific concerns in the respective countries.

Thus, they serve as powerful case studies for identifying successes and limitations. The test cases shed light on the importance of paying attention to the institutional and cultural setting in which future JG programs may be developed. The fundamental key to a successful JG program is to create programs that both employ people and benefit local communities.

Many continue to argue that, through direct job creation, sustainable full employment is within reach (Darity and Hamilton, 2012). The JG programs discussed in the present volume provide economists, researchers, and policymakers with a starting point to address the global problem of unemployment and underemployment. Even several years after the formal end of the "Great Recession," global unemployment and underemployment remain stuck at high rates. The need for serious consideration of job creation policies has never been greater since the Great Depression.

Note

1. A notable exception is the case study of Argentina; see Tcherneva and Wray (2005a) and (2005b).

References

Darity, Jr., William and Darrick Hamilton (2012). "Bold Policies for Economic Justice," *Review of Black Political Economy*, 39: 79–85.

Forstater, Mathew (2004). "Green Jobs: Addressing the Critical Issues Surrounding the Environment, Workplace and Employment," *International Journal of Environment, Workplace and Employment*, 1(1): 53–61.

Minsky, Hyman P. (1986). *Stabilizing an Unstable Economy*, New Haven: CT, Yale University Press.

Murray, Michael J. and Mathew Forstater (2013). *The Job Guarantee: Toward True Full Employment*, New York: Palgrave Macmillan.

Nell, Edward J., Majewski, Ray, and Murray, Michael J. (2012). *Maintaining Full Employment*, Manuscript.

Rose, Nancy E. (1994). *Put to Work: The WPA and Public Employment in the Great Depression*, New York: Monthly Review Press.

Tcherneva, Pavlina R. and Wray, L. Randall (2005a). "Is Argentina's *Jefes de Hogar* an Employer of Last Resort Program?," *Working Paper 43*, Center for Full Employment and Price Stability, University of Missouri—Kansas City.

Tcherneva, Pavlina R. and Wray, L. Randall (2005b). "Employer of Last Resort: A Case Study of Argentina's *Jefes* Program," *Working Paper 41*, Center for Full Employment and Price Stability, University of Missouri—Kansas City.

CHAPTER 1

Green Jobs for Full Employment, a Stock Flow Consistent Analysis

Antoine Godin

Guaranteed Job and the Kyoto Protocol

Unemployment is a fact in present economies. Even without a crisis, unemployment exists and costs a lot to society. Reasons for unemployment are multiple and differ according to the theory at hand. Lack of effective demand, imperfect markets, and friction are examples of unemployment justifications. All sorts of policies based on these different theories have been implemented with varying results but none have proven effective in tackling unemployment. Full employment has never been achieved during the last 40 years. Often the problem is that these policies promote indirect jobs creation: public spending, wage subsidies, incentives, tax cuts, job training. Another issue is the change in the dimension of these policies; we now have microeconomic supply of labor policies instead of macroeconomic demand stimulation policies. Even if they meet some objectives, these policies do not provide an answer to unemployment.

It is the duty of the state, as Lerner expressed it, to provide jobs when the market fails to do so (Lerner, 1944, 1951). By guaranteeing a job to all that are willing and able to work, the state would remove all involuntary unemployment. Examples of such job guarantee schemes exist, even if they have never been developed on a full scale.[1] Furthermore, in most economies the potential of energy saving via insulation and uses that are more efficient is important. In order to reach the Kyoto Protocol objectives, it is urgent to develop policies that reduce the production of carbon dioxide.

This chapter presents a stock flow consistent (SFC) model of a multisectorial economy with an Employer of Last Resort (ELR) scheme where ELR workers would work to transform the economy toward a greener one. We will focus on the impact of the green job ELR policy and compare these results with a standard Keynesian demand spur (KDS).

Overview of the Model

SFC models are based on the works of two schools of thoughts developed by Wynne Godley and James Tobin. Both these approaches are centered on the importance of consistency between and among stocks and flows: each flow in the model comes from a sector (or account) and goes to another account. In each period, the sum of flows has to be nil. Stocks are the sum of inflows and outflows. SFC models are thus evolutionary models (Godley and Lavoie, 2007).

The economy modeled in this chapter discusses two household sectors (wage earners and capitalists), three productive sectors (capital goods, energy, and widgets), a banking sector, and a public sector. Figure 1.1 represents the flow diagram of the model. Both household sectors and the public sector consume widgets and electricity (thin dashed lines on the diagram). Furthermore, all productive sectors consume energy to produce their own goods. All productive sectors use fixed capital (produced by the capital goods sector, thin dash-dotted line) and labor (thick solid line). In order to invest, firms borrow money from banks and pay interests (thick dotted line). Finally, industries pay wages to workers (thick solid line) and dividends to capitalists (thick dashed line). Household sectors save part of their wealth as cash on their current account (thin solid lines) and as bonds (thick dash-dotted lines) for which they receive interests. Banks balance their liabilities (current accounts) with loans to firms and by bond holding (thin dotted line) for which they receive interests. The government imposes a tax on wages and profits (thick dash-dotted lines), pays interests on bonds, and gives a dole to unemployed workers.

The chapter is structured as follows. The second section will analyze structural unemployment and the policies implemented in order to reduce it. The third and fourth sections will present the multisectorial model and

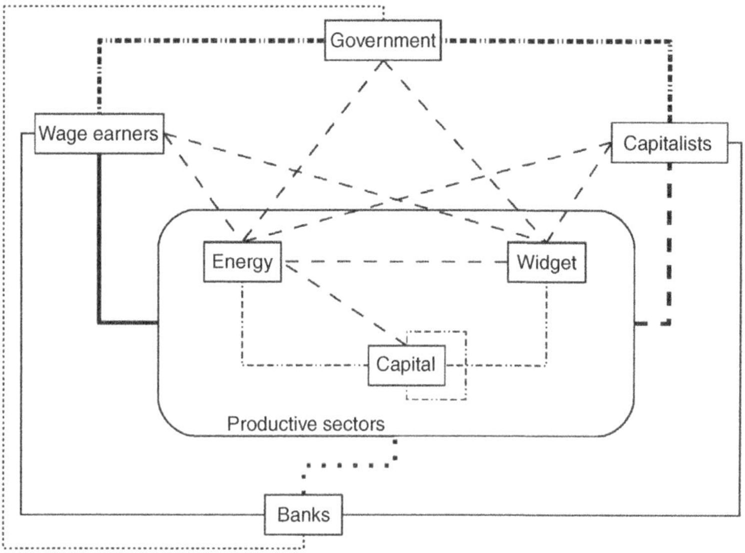

Figure 1.1 Flow diagram. Each line represents a group of flows between two sectors. Each group of flow might be bidirectional. For example, the line linking wage earners and government represents flows from wage earners to government (taxes, bond holding) and flows from government to wage earners (dole, interests on bonds)

its steady state. The ELR scheme and its impacts are studied in the fifth section. Finally, the sixth section provides the conclusion.

Unemployment

Mainstream economics usually explains unemployment by market rigidities. Unemployment would disappear if wages were allowed to decline low enough. Labor market is like all other good markets with rigid price and should not be seen as anything else. However, unemployment is not often recognized for the function it has in a capitalist economy (Forstater, 1998, 2006). Most of the time, firms are working with excess capacity in order to be able to respond to sudden changes in demand. Unemployment thus allows the economy to be more flexible by permitting firms to hire workers out of the "reserve army of labor" when needed.

Following Schumpeterian *creative destruction,* the process of birth of new technologies creates unemployment in obsolete sectors while creating jobs in new sectors (Schumpeter, 1934/1912). Structural unemployment may also be explained as a mismatch between demand and supply. Pasinetti (1993) shows it is highly improbable that, in a multisectorial model, distribution of demand among different sectors is such that full employment prevails, even when aggregate demand is high enough to imply full employment.

Ros (2000) explains using various two-sector models that labor surplus economies arise for different reasons. He uses efficiency wages on top of a Lewis growth model to show how Kaldorian underemployment appears.[2] In Chapter 11, he also shows how unemployment emerges out of constrained economies, using a Kaleckian dual economy model.

It is illusionary to assume that capitalist economies will ever attain full employment under a normal situation.[3] The only period of time in the modern era where full employment was reached in the United States is during World War II (Kaboub, 2007). Kaboub further adds, "Full employment and price stability were achieved, but only during wartime with a considerable number of the male working-age adults being in the army and the rest of the working-age population employed to support the war effort. Therefore, the US full employment experiment must be taken with caution" (Kaboub, 2007, p. 4). In March 1999, US unemployment reached its lowest since the 1960s and was considered as "full employment." It was then at 4.2 percent, clearly showing that full employment was never reached in the postwar period.

Furthermore, not only is full employment not likely to be achieved but employment also follows business cycles. Indeed, lack of aggregate demand during crisis leads to higher levels of unemployment, as Keynes (1936) explained in his *General Theory of Employment, Interest and Money.* All of the components of effective demand are highly sensitive to expectations that are depressed during tough times. Therefore, not only is it improbable to attain full employment because of *structural* unemployment, it is also doubtful that it is maintained due to *cyclical* unemployment (Forstater, 2003).

The policy space for employment policies is thus large and important and needs commitment. "Unemployment cannot be conquered by a democracy until it is understood. Full productive employment in a free society is possible but it is not possible without taking pains. It cannot be won by waving a financial wand: it is a goal that can be reached only by conscious continuous organization of all our productive resources under democratic control. To win full employment and keep it, we must will the end and must understand and will the means" (Beveridge, 1945, in [Papadimitriou, 1999]).

Employment Policies

Full employment was the objective of employment policies in the post–World War II period until the mid-70s. Then, we observed a switch in the goal of employment policies. We went from what Mitchell and Muyskens (2008) call a *Full Employment Framework* to a *Full Employability Framework*.[4] Employment is now seen as a microeconomic problem. Employment policies are not macroeconomic or Keynesian aggregate demand spur anymore. They are now designed as microeconomic and supply side.

According to the Full Employability Framework, unemployed workers are unemployed because they are not attractive enough and they need to be more "sexy" in order to find a job. Active Labor Market Policies (ALMP) are examples of these micropolicies. The effectiveness of ALMP is not encouraging according to de Koning (2001) and Martin (1998). However, Martin stresses their potential role in fighting high and persistent unemployment while de Koning underlines the increasing need for these policies in the future.

On the macroeconomic side, the "fit all" solution is growth: in order to have more jobs, an economy needs to grow. According to Minsky, focusing on pro-growth rather than employment policies is a mistake since a fully employed economy is bound to grow while a growing economy might not be at full employment (Minsky, 1986). Indeed, correlation between employment growth and GDP growth are mixed as table 1.1 shows.

Table 1.1 Correlation between GDP growth and employment growth is varying from not correlated at all (United Kingdom, Turkey) to slightly correlated (Chile, Japan) to strongly correlated (United States)

	Correlation
Australia (1965–2010)	0,16
Chile (1987–2010)	0,48
Germany (1970–2010)	0,14
Italy (1970–2010)	0,20
Japan (1970 2010)	0,60
Turkey (1970–2010)	0,10
United Kingdom (1970–2010)	0,05
United States (1970–2010)	0,77

Sources: OECD (2011).

What emerges from effectiveness analysis of present employment policies is that, even if some have interesting results, none of them have achieved the low unemployment level of the post–World War II period. Furthermore, these policies do not aim at full employment anymore but at maximum employment possible under present conditions. We need a change in employment policies such that full employment again becomes the target of these policies.

A Role for the Government

Market economy only chooses to produce what has a price and what is profitable to the producer. As Lunghini puts it, "Production of goods stops not when needs are satisfied but when profits realization imposes it" (Lunghini, 1995, *my translation*). Thus, a good without a price would not be produced since no monetary profits can be extracted from it. What is more, some needs will never be satisfied by an economy that is only interested in what is profitable. Entire sectors of the economy would not exist if it were not for government programs and policies.

Also, governments might have a better vision of which is the best direction of the economy for the benefit of all. Climate change is a good example of such cases. We thus need a government to be able to influence the structure of the economy and drive it to what would be more profitable for all[5] (Forstater, 1998; Mitchell, 2007).

Besides, Forstater (1998) notes that increased private-sector activity can lead to bottlenecks or inflationary pressure due to excess capacity utilization or resource depletion. Indeed, because of structural rigidities of the economy or competitive pressures, private-sector firms may chose not to change technology or to engage in natural resource-intensive means of production without observing the negative externalities it would imply. Governments, being free of these rigidities or pressures, are thus more able to conduct structural changes. According to Lerner (1951), we cannot trust the people to drive the economy correctly because, even if they know the consequences of their acts, they will misbehave if it is in their own interest. Consequently, there is a need for the state to take over the steering wheel of the economy. For example, "investments can be undertaken by the governments which show a money loss but which are considered worthwhile in the social interest because they yield benefits other than those which result in a money income" (Lerner, 1951, p. 91). Finally, Keynes stresses the importance of public investments pointing "that a somewhat comprehensive socialisation of investment will prove the only means of securing an approximation to full employment" (Keynes, 1936, p. 378).

A Multisectorial SFC Model

Stock Flow Consistency in a Nutshell

The SFC approach is a very active strand of the post-Keynesian literature. As SFC models are nominal models, they are well fitted to analyze financial-real interactions, with some authors such as Lavoie and Godley (2001–2002), Dos Santos and Zezza (2004, 2006, 2008), Dos Santos and Macedo e Silva (2009), Foley and Taylor (2006), among others, working on growth and distribution models. SFC models may also be used to analyze investment decisions such as in Chatelain (2010). Others use agent-based SFC models (see Kinsella et al. 2011; Seppecher 2012). Finally Passarella (2012), among others, use Minskian SFC models to analyze financial instability.

The economy presented here comprises two household sectors, that is, wage earners and capitalists; three production industries, that is, energy, investment, and widget; and one public sector. Intermediate goods are not discussed for each of these industries. However, some goods produced in one industry serve as inputs for other industries.[6]

Only three industries are modeled. Godley and Lavoie (2007), often discussing only one production sector, justify this assumption for the sake of simplicity. Lee (1998) criticizes this choice pointing to the lack of pricing interdependencies. This critique does not apply to our model since we will be able to observe some pricing interdependence as the three productive sectors are using output of other industries as input for their own production.

Structure of the Model

Table 1.2 is the Social Account Matrix (SAM) of the economy.[7] It shows how flows circulate in the economy. SAM allows seeing what are the earnings (row) and spending (column) of each sector. For example, the first row shows that earnings from the energy sector comprises consumption from the widget sector ($C_{w,e}$) and the capital goods sector ($C_{i,e}$), from both household sectors ($C_{h,e}$ and $C_{ca,e}$) and from the public sector ($C_{g,e}$), while the first column reveals that the energy sector spends all its income in investments (I_e), wages ($N_e W_e$), profits (F_e), and interests ($r_l L_{e,-1}$).

Table 1.2 Social Account Matrix (SAM)

	Energy	*Widget*	*Cap. Goods*	*Wage earners*	*Capitalists*	*Government*	*Banks*	*Total*
Energy		$C_{w,e}$	$C_{i,e}$	$C_{h,e}$	$C_{ca,e}$	$C_{g,e}$	$+\Delta L_e$	Y_e
Widget				$C_{h,w}$	$C_{ca,w}$	$C_{g,w}$	$+\Delta L_w$	Y_w
Capital Goods	I_e	I_w	I_i				$+\Delta L_i$	Y_i
Wage earners	$N_e W_e$	$N_w W_w$	$N_i W_i$			$G_T U + r_b B_{h,-1}$		Y_h
Capitalists	F_e	F_w	F_i			$r_b B_{ca,-1}$	F_b	Y_{ca}
Government				$T_h + \Delta B_h$	$T_{ca} + \Delta B_{ca}$		ΔB_b	$T + \Delta B$
Banks	$r_l L_{e,-1}$	$r_l L_{w,-1}$	$r_l L_{i,-1}$	$+\Delta M_h$	$+\Delta M_{ca}$	$r_b B_{b,-1}$		Y_b
Total	Y_e	Y_w	Y_i	Y_h	Y_{ca}	G	Y_b	

Table 1.3 is the balance sheet. It represents how stocks are distributed among the different sectors. It shows that the net worth of firms is equal to zero as all their wealth is transferred to capitalists. It also indicates that banks have no net worth as they use bond holding to balance their liabilities and assets. Private wealth thus consists of financial wealth (cash and bonds) from households and real wealth (firms net worth) from capitalists' households. Financial private net worth is balanced by public net worth as shown by the Balance row of the balance sheet.

The Transaction Flow Matrix (TFM, table 1.4) ensures that the sum of all flows is always nil. A plus sign expresses an inflow while a minus sign represents an outflow. For instance, the fourth row shows that wages are paid by the three productive sectors to wage earners and thus come with a minus sign in the Energy column and with a plus sign in the Wage Earners sector. From the tables we can see that profits are distributed to the capitalist class. Household sectors consume both energy and widgets, pay taxes (T_h and T_{ca}), and save everything left either as bonds (ΔB_h and ΔB_{ca}) or as cash (ΔM_h and ΔM_{ca}). Banks hold deposits from both kinds of households and receive interests for the loans accorded to firms and from the bonds they hold. Finally, government, seen here as both the government and the central bank, consumes both energy and widgets, transfers san unemployment benefits (G_T) to jobless wage earners, and pays interests to bonds holders. The change in stock is represented in the second part of the TFM.

The following subsections describe the model; a complete list of all the equations of the model can be found in Appendix B.

Household Sectors

Wage Earners

Wage earners offer their labor for a salary and receive a dole when unemployed. Furthermore, they perceive interests for their bond holding. Their aggregated nominal disposable income is thus composed of the wage bill minus taxes, of the unemployment benefits, and of interests on bonds. We assume nominal wages and unemployment benefits fixed, as we are not interested in inflation processes.

We suppose that wage earners construct a consumer price index and an inflation rate based on their preferences and on prices of energy and widgets. We then define a real disposable income based on Haig-Simons' definition[8] in order to determine their consumption level.

Table 1.3 Balance sheet

	Energy	*Widget*	*Capital goods*	*Wage earners*	*Capitalists*	*Government*	*Banks*	Σ
Fixed Capital	$+K_e$	$+K_w$	$+K_i$					$+K$
Cash				$+M_h$	$+M_{ca}$		$-M$	0
Bonds				$+B_h$	$+B_{ca}$	$-B$	$+B_b$	0
Loans	$-L_e$	$-L_w$	$-L_i$				$+L$	0
Owned Firms	$-VK_e$	$-VK_w$	$-VK_i$		$+VK$			0
Balance	0	0	0	$-V_h$	$-V_{ca}$	$+V_g$	0	$-V$
Σ	0	0	0	0	0	0	0	0

Table 1.4 Transaction Flow Matrix

	Energy		Widget		Investment		Wage Earners	Capitalists	Government	Bank		Σ
	Current	*Capital*	*Current*	*Capital*	*Current*	*Capital*				*Current*	*Capital*	
Consumption			$+C_w$				$-C_{h,w}$	$-C_{ca,w}$	$-C_{g,w}$			0
Energy	$+C_e$		$-C_{w,e}$		$-C_{i,e}$		$-C_{h,e}$	$-C_{ca,e}$	$-C_{g,e}$			0
Investments		$-I_e$		$-I_w$	$+I$	$-I_i$						0
Wages	$-W_eN_e$		$-W_wN_w$		$-W_iN_i$		$+WB$					0
Retained Earnings	$-RE_e$	$+RE_e$	$-RE_w$	$+RE_w$	$-RE_i$	$+RE_i$						0
Profits	$-F_e$		$-F_w$		$-F_i$			$+F$		$-F_b$		0
Loan Interest	$-r_lL_{e,-1}$		$-r_lL_{w,-1}$		$-r_lL_{i,-1}$							
Bond Interests							$+r_bB_{h,-1}$	$+r_bB_{ca,-1}$	$-r_bB_{-1}$	$+r_bB_{b,-1}$		0
Transfers							$+G_TU$		$-G_TU$			0
Taxes							$-T_h$	$-T_{ca}$	$+T$			0
Change in loans		$+\Delta L_e$		$+\Delta L_w$		$+\Delta L_i$					$-\Delta L$	0
Change in deposits							$-\Delta M_h$	$-\Delta M_{ca}$			$+\Delta M$	0
Change in bonds							$-\Delta B_h$	$-\Delta B_{ca}$	$+\Delta B$		$-\Delta B_b$	0
Change in net worth		$+\Delta VK_e$		$+\Delta VK_w$		$+\Delta VK_i$		$-\Delta VK$				0
Σ	0	0	0	0	0	0	0	0	0	0	0	0

Total real consumption is a function of Haig-Simons' real disposable income and real wealth in the previous period. Wage earners' consumptions of energy and widget is determined through a Linear Expenditure System (LES) reflecting their preferences over energy and widget and according to relative prices and minimum consumption of both goods.

All disposable income that is not consumed is saved. Wage earners face a portfolio decision, as they have to choose to hold their wealth as bonds or as cash. They choose their desired holding of bonds based on previous stock of wealth and interest rate on bonds. Cash holding is then equal to residual wealth (i.e., nominal wealth minus bond holding).

Capitalists

Capitalists' aggregate disposable income is composed of profits from all productive sectors and banks, minus taxes plus interests from bonds. As wage earners, capitalists consume both energy and widgets and save all income that is not spent as cash. Wealth of capitalists consists of their financial wealth (cash and bonds) and firms' net wealth since capitalists own them. As a consequence, firms' wealth will affect the consumption decision of capitalists.[9] Portfolio choice for capitalists is based on financial wealth only and not on total wealth.

Production Sectors

Demand

All production sectors are demand-driven. They all need fixed capital stock in order to produce. Because we assume integrated sectors, there are no intermediate goods and each output is net output. However, all productive sectors need electricity in order to produce their respective goods. Sectorial demands in electricity are determined through energy productivity in each industry. The energy sector has a demand equal to household consumption plus demand from the two other productive sectors and from the public sector. Aggregate demand for widget is equal to households' and government's desired consumption. Demand in the capital good industry comprises investment from the three productive sectors. Capital stock level determines maximum output to be produced in each period.

Employment

Employment in each sector is demand-determined through sectorial productivity. Firms assume as many workers they need to produce enough goods to satisfy the demand they face. We assume perfect mobility of labor and no differentiation of workers. Firms hire workers from the labor force up to the level of employment they need. Unemployment is equal to the difference between labor force and aggregate employment.

Investments

Desired capital growth (g_k, 1) is a function of *actual* capacity utilization[10] (u) and *targeted* capacity utilization (u^T).[11] Capacity utilization (2) is defined as the ratio of actual output (y) and practical[12] full capacity output (y_{fc}), which is computed through (3) where pr_k is capital productivity under normal conditions. Real investment is equal to desired capital growth plus depreciation rate but cannot be negative (4).

$$g_k = \gamma_0 + \gamma_1(u_{-1} - u^T) \tag{1}$$

$$u = \frac{y}{y_{fc}} \tag{2}$$

$$y_{fc} = k.pr_k \tag{3}$$

$$i = Max[g_k + \delta, 0]\, k_{-1} \tag{4}$$

$$\Delta k = i - \delta.k_{-1} \tag{5}$$

Costs

Unit costs are a decreasing linear function of output (y), for a given stock of capital (k) and a given stock of debt (L),[13] up to the level of practical full capacity. After that point, unit costs are a quadratic increasing function of output until *technical* full capacity (Lavoie, 1992).[14]

$$UC(y) = \begin{cases} \dfrac{W}{pr_n} + \dfrac{\delta.k + r_l L_{-1}}{y} & if \quad u \leq 1 \\ \beta + \alpha(y - y_{fc})^2 & if \quad u > 1 \end{cases} \tag{6}$$

where $\frac{W}{pr_n}$ are the labor unit costs. From (1) and (4), we observe that when $u < u^T - \frac{\delta + \gamma_0}{\gamma_1} = u_{\min}$, firms are not replacing depreciated capital. The unit cost function is thus modified in order to reflect this choice:

$$UC(y) = \begin{cases} \frac{W}{pr_n} + \frac{r_l L_{-1}}{y} & if \quad u < u_{\min} \\ \frac{W}{pr_n} + \frac{\delta.k + r_l L_{-1}}{y} & if \quad u_{\min} < u < 1 \\ \beta + \alpha(y - y_{fc})^2 & if \quad u > 1 \end{cases} \tag{7}$$

Prices

Prices are Kaleckian markup prices based on unit cost.[15] The markup is used to generate profits, which are then divided in two. The first part of profits is distributed to shareholders as dividends; the second part is used to finance investments or to repay loans. For explicative purposes, the markup is thus divided in two: $\tau = \theta + \phi.\theta$ is the part of the markup related to dividends, while ϕ is the part of market related to investments.

$$p = (1 + \theta + \phi)\, UC(y^e) \tag{8}$$

Dividends are assumed to be targeted such that they are equal to the desired return on capital r_s times the capital stock (9), based on expected sales y^e and expected unit costs $UC(y^e)$ (10).

$$F = r_s p_{k,-1} k_{-1} \tag{9}$$

$$\theta = \frac{r_s p_{k,-1} k_{-1}}{UC(y^e)\, y^e} \tag{10}$$

Kalecki (1971) shows that a fraction ρ of retained earnings (*RE*) can be borrowed to finance investments. When firms decide to invest, they need to generate sufficient retained earnings in order to finance their desired level of investments. Furthermore, we assume that firms are targeting a fixed level of leverage (λ^T). Given the level of investment (4), the actual level of leverage (λ, 11), and targeted level of leverage, firms decide what fraction of nominal investment is to be borrowed (12). In the case where it is not possible to reach the targeted level of leverage given the desired investment (and thus ρ should be negative), we assume that firms use retained earnings not only to finance investment but also to repay loans. Targeted retained earnings being determined by (13), the markup ϕ is determined through (14).

$$\lambda = \frac{L}{p_k k} \tag{11}$$

$$\rho = \frac{L}{p_k k} \tag{12}$$

$$RE^e = \phi UC(y^e) y^e \tag{13}$$

$$\phi = \frac{g_k k . p_k}{(1+\rho)\, UC(y^e)\, y^e} + z \frac{L - \lambda^T p_k k + i}{UC(y^e)\, y^e} \tag{14}$$

$$z = 1 \quad if \quad \rho = 0 \tag{15}$$

Expected sales growth is inversely proportional to price inflation (16).

$$y^e = y_{-1}(1 - \hat{p}) \tag{16}$$

Figure 1.2 summarizes the pricing decision that firms face. The blue line represents expected sales as a function of price. The purple line represents needed sales for a given price so that the firm is able to finance investment and debt repayment. The intersections of the two lines are possible prices such that retained earnings are equal to their desired level. If the level of

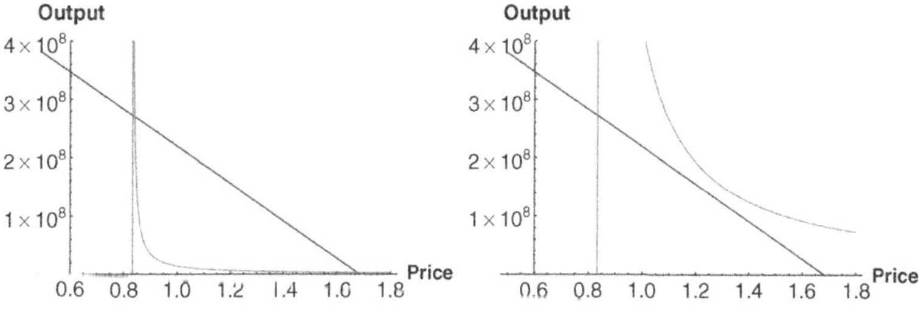

Figure 1.2 Firms' pricing decision. The black line represents expected sales as a function of price. The gray line represents desired sales for a given price in order to be able to finance investment and debt repayment. The intersections of the two lines are possible prices such that retained earnings meet its desired level

desired retained earnings is low enough (case a), then there are one or two possible prices, one that maximizes output and one that maximizes prices. We assume that firms always choose the output maximizing solution. However, there are cases where, given the desired level of retained earnings, there is no solution to the system (case b). Firms then have to lower their desired level of retained earnings.

Finance

Variation in loans (18) is equal to nominal investments minus realized retained earnings (17). Net wealth of firms is equal to tangible assets minus liabilities (19).

$$RE = (p - UC(y))y - F \tag{17}$$

$$\Delta L = p_k i - RE \tag{18}$$

$$V = p_k k - L \tag{19}$$

Banking Sector

Banks are not supposed to hold any cash reserves; the stock of deposits is equal to the stock of loans to firms plus the stock of government bonds. We assume that banks respond positively to all loan demand and that loans are always repaid. Bonds' holding is then a residual choice. Profits are made of interests from loans and bonds.

Government Sector

Public-sector income is given by tax receipt while expenditures consist of energy consumption, widget consumption, and unemployment subsidies. We assume, at first and with no loss of generality, fixed total nominal public consumption of energy and widget. Households and banks determine bond demand while bond supply is equal to the budget deficit.

Steady State

As the model is static, a steady state is reached when variations in stocks are all nil. For the capital stock to be constant, growth in capital has to be nil, in which case investment is equal to capital depreciation.

Furthermore, leverage level has to have reached its targeted value. Hence when capacity utilization and leverage level have reached their steady-state value, a system of equations depending on various parameters and the level of capacity utilization determines prices.[16]

In order to find steady-state levels of capital stock, wealth, disposable income, and so on, other observations are needed. At the steady state, household wealth is constant. Besides, inflation is nil. All income is spent and income is equal to a fraction of wealth. Bond and cash holdings are also constant. This determines a second system of equation.

From these two systems of equations, it is interesting to note that prices depend only on targeted values of capacity utilization and leverage level and on technical and financial parameters such as productivity, depreciation, interest, and return rates. Furthermore, the role of a few essential parameters may be observed. These parameters represent key behavioral elements. Influencing those behaviors could impact aggregate indicators such as employment, income, or poverty. This underlines the multiplicity of means in order to attain certain goals.

First of all, the leverage level (λ) and the capacity utilization rate (u) have a redistributive effect between capitalists and wage earners, as figure 1.3 shows. The leverage level (λ) has a positive impact on capitalists' income. Furthermore, a decrease in capacity utilization also increases capitalists' income through an increase in capital stock and thus on return on capital for the same output. Both these parameters have only a small direct impact on wage earners' income. What is more, both these parameters

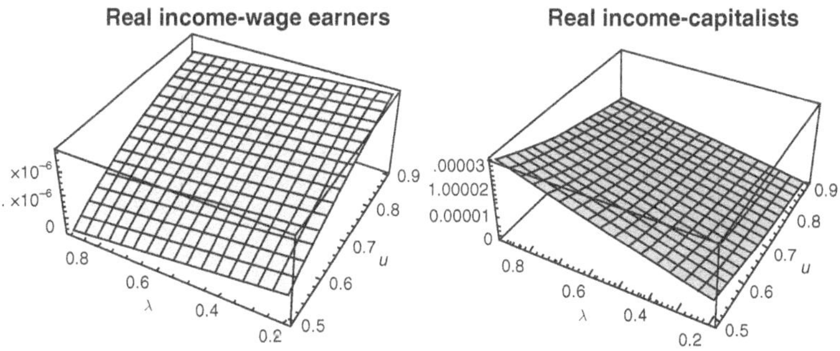

Figure 1.3 The redistributive effect of leverage level (λ) and capacity utilization (u). Increased leverage increases capitalists' income and decreases wage earners' income. Lower capacity utilization increases capitalists' income and decreases wage earners' income

have a positive impact on prices and thus reduce real wages of workers. On the aggregate, the leverage level and the capacity utilization have a light impact on employment (higher leverage and lower capacity imply higher unemployment) and on debt to GDP ratio (higher leverage and higher capacity imply higher debt to GDP ratio).

The second interesting pair of parameters to analyze is the interest rate on bond holding (r_b) and the level of government consumption ($CG = C_{g,e} + C_{g,i}$) and is described in figure 1.4, which illustrates the impacts that these parameters have on unemployment and on debt to GDP ratio. The interest rate on bonds has an obvious income effect for all households but it also has an impact on the quantity of bonds held, which increases even more income. This increased bond holding level has a direct effect on debt to GDP ratio since the debt level is equal to bond supply. Due to the income increase that the interest rate on bonds has, consumption increase with r_b implies a reduction in unemployment. Government consumption has a mild negative effect on debt to GDP ratio. It is negative since the Keynesian multiplier on government spending is higher than one. The level of steady-state debt depends slightly on government spending, since debt depends on desired bonds holding by households and banks. Because an increased level of government consumption implies an increase in income for all household sectors, it also implies a higher level of wealth and thus a higher level of bond holding. On the other hand, government spending has a strong impact on unemployment. This is the standard KDS that will be analyzed in more depth.

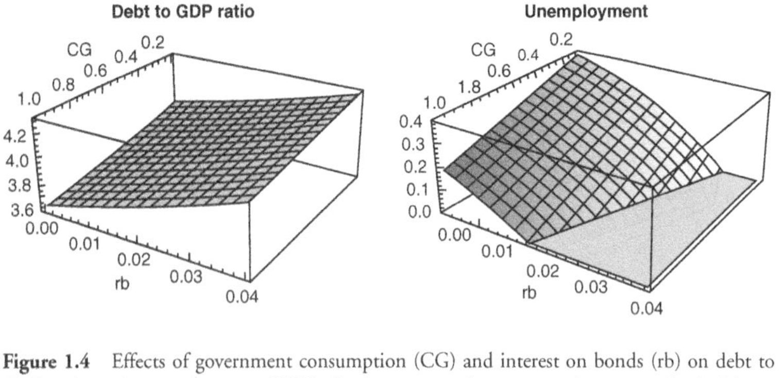

Figure 1.4 Effects of government consumption (CG) and interest on bonds (rb) on debt to GDP ratio and unemployment. While the interest rate has a strong impact on both debt to GDP ratio and unemployment, public consumption surprisingly has little effect on public debt. However, public spending strongly impacts unemployment through a demand spur

Green Jobs

Literature on cost-benefit analysis of green buildings is wide. Clinch and Healy (2001); Hens and Verdonck (2001); Levine et al. (2007); of Science and Technology (2005) focus on domestic houses while others focus on public buildings Kats et al. (2005); Kats (2006); Xenergy Inc and Sera Architects (2000). Generally, various benefits are cited: energy and water savings, improved health and decreased mortality, enhanced student learning, increased productivity, job creation, all leading to clear economic and social profits.[17] We will only consider energy savings both in dwellings and in public buildings.

Adding the ELR in the Model

Introducing a green job ELR in the economy does not change the model much. Table 1.5 is the Social Account Matrix. The only difference from the previous model is that now unemployed workers do not receive an unemployment subsidy but are employed by the state for a minimum wage. The balance sheet does not change and as such is not reproduced here.

Equations Modifications

There are no substantial modifications. First of all, as already stated, wage earners' income now comprises private-sector earnings and ELR wage instead of the dole. Second, works done under ELR have an effect both on governmental and on household energy consumption. Equation (20) shows that we relax the hypothesis of constant government spending, as public energy consumption decreases proportionally to the size of ELR (measured by u, the private unemployment rate). Equation (21) indicates that wage earners' propensity to consume energy (β_h) also diminishes proportionally to the ELR size.

$$C_{g,e} = (1 - \xi_g u)\, C_{g,e,-1} \tag{20}$$

$$\beta_h = (1 - \xi_h u)\, \beta_{h,-1} \tag{21}$$

Green job ELR versus Baseline

The first set of simulations[18] analyzes the structural effect of a green job ELR scheme (hereafter GJ) on the economy. The GJ starts in period 25.

Table 1.5 ELR Social Account Matrix

	Energy	*Widget*	*Cap. Goods*	*Wage earners*	*Capitalists*	*Government*	*Banks*	*Total*
Energy		$C_{w,e}$	$C_{i,e}$	$C_{h,e}$	$C_{ca,e}$	$C_{g,e}$	$+\Delta L_e$	Y_e
Widget				$C_{h,w}$	$C_{ca,w}$	$C_{g,w}$	$+\Delta L_w$	Y_w
Capital Goods	I_e	I_w	I_i				$+\Delta L_i$	Y_i
Wage earners	$N_e W_e$	$N_w W_w$	$N_i W_i$			$UW_{ELR} + r_b B_{h,-1}$		Y_h
Capitalists	F_e	F_w	F_i			$r_b B_{ca,-1}$	F_b	Y_{ca}
Government				$T_h + \Delta B_h$	$T_{ca} + \Delta B_{ca}$		ΔB_b	$T + \Delta B$
Banks	$r_l L_{e,-1}$	$r_l L_{w,-1}$	$r_l L_{i,-1}$	$+\Delta M_h$	$+\Delta M_{ca}$	$r_b B_{b,-1}$		Y_b
Total	Y_e	Y_w	Y_i	Y_h	Y_{ca}	G	Y_b	

The policy consists of an expected increase of total government spending of 10 percent, an increase that is devoted to the wage paid to ELR workers.[19] Furthermore, ELR changes the consumption patterns of both wage earners and the public sector following (20) and (21). It is important to note that since these two equations constantly modify the parameters, no steady state can be reached. The economy is constantly changing according to the new preferences of wage earners as well as to the new government spending.

Figure 1.5 shows the results obtained through these simulations. In all graphs, the blue line represents the Green job ELR results while the red line represents the baseline ones. All the results are relative changes from steady-state values.

Obviously, unemployment disappears as soon as ELR is put into action. However, not all workers are employed in the private sector. The analysis is conducted on how *private unemployment* (i.e., all workers not employed in the private sector, that is, ELR workers) varies. Figure 1.5 shows that private unemployment decreases directly by almost 15 percent. Then, due to the structural change that green jobs imply, private unemployment keeps decreasing rather steeply at first and then more gently. This decreasing unemployment depends on whether the energy sector is more or less labor-intensive than the consumption goods industry. It is also interesting to note that the predicted 10 percent increase in government spending is not reached at all. Private unemployment decreases drastically due to the increase in aggregate consumption from both household sectors, lowering the cost of ELR.

Both household sectors see an increase in their income after the green job program is enacted. This leads to an increase in their wealth resulting in an increase in desired bond holding. This implies an increase in the public debt level. Furthermore, GDP also increases, due to an increase in consumption and investments. The increase in public debt is, nonetheless, larger than the increase in GDP leading to an increased level of debt to GDP of about 0.4 percent. The 6 percent increase in government expenditure observed at the beginning of the program is lowered as private unemployment keeps decreasing, removing workers out of ELR, and as public energy consumption decreases.

The structural change in the economy can be observed through employment in widget and energy production sectors. In the short run, the increase in income by both wage earners and capitalists increases energy consumption. In the long run, the reduction in energy consumption by both the public sector and wage earners leads to a reduction

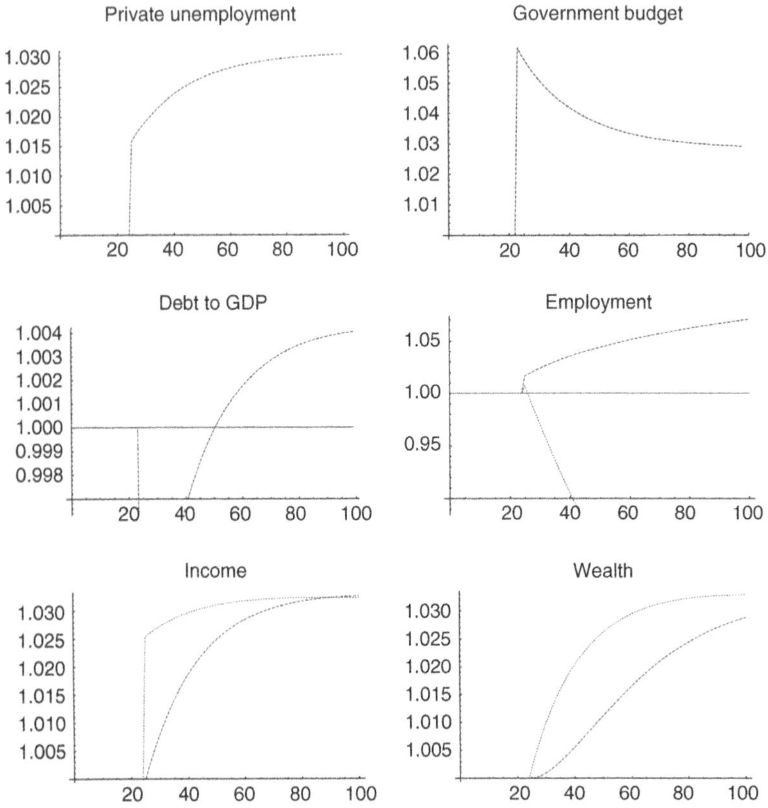

Figure 1.5 Green Job (GJ, dashed, dotted) vs baseline (solid) scenarios. Private unemployment decreases drastically after enabling the GJ scheme. Government spending increases by around 6 percent. The debt to GDP ratio has a sudden variation right after enacting GJ but then stabilizes at a level 4 percent above the baseline case. The structural change in the economy can be observed in the employment level in both widget (dashed line) and energy (dotted line) production sectors. While employment in the widget sector increases, it decreases in the energy industry. Both income and wealth increase for wage earners (dashed lines) and capitalists (dotted lines)

in energy consumption. This leads to a reduction in employment in the energy industry. However, the reduction in energy employment is countered by an increase in the widget sector.[20]

Three conclusions can be drawn from this analysis. First, an ELR is a direct way to remove all involuntary unemployment and address poverty issues. Second, a green job ELR implies structural changes in the economy aiming at lower energy consumption. Regarding the structural change, the present model does not include synergy effects that a green job public sector might imply. It is obvious that imitative firms would appear on the market as soon as new green technologies would be used in the green job program. Finally, aggregate ELR cost has to be lowered by the reduction in unemployment due to the spur in aggregate demand that higher income implies. In our simulation, a predicted 10 percent increase in government spending leads to an ex-post increase of only 4 percent. Furthermore, poor people usually receive benefits, which could be removed for ELR workers, further lowering the cost of ELR.

Employer of Last Resort versus Keynesian Demand Spur

The second set of simulation analyzes the effects of two employment policies: the "traditional" KDS through increased government spending and an ELR scheme. In this analysis, the structural effect of ELR through energy saving (20) and (21) is not implemented in order to analyze only the employment effect through a new steady-state reach.[21] The two simulations are conducted in the same way: at time 25, the policy is enacted. The policies consist of a realized increase of total government spending of 6 percent, an increase that is devoted either to increase in both energy and widget consumption (in the KDS case) or to the wage paid to unemployed workers (in the ELR case).

Figure 1.6 shows the results obtained for these simulations. In all graphs, the blue line represents the ELR results while the red line represents KDS ones. All the results are relative changes from steady-state values.

Evidently, the impact of the KDS on GDP is stronger as the whole increase in government budget is directly used to increase production while in the case of ELR, part of that increase is saved by ELR workers. Furthermore, the Keynesian multiplier on public spending is higher than one. The debt to GDP ratio is thus lower in the KDS case; it is even lower than before the policy is enacted. Since GDP increases more in the KDS case (4.5 percent) than in the ELR case (3 percent), private unemployment decreases more in the first case than in the second (30 percent reduction versus 15 percent reduction). In the ELR case, however, involuntary unemployment is totally removed since the green job program hires privately unemployed workers.

An interesting point is with regard to income and wealth of all household sectors. Both income and wealth increase more in the ELR case (blue line) than in the KDS case (red line). At first, the impact is stronger on wage earners' (solid lines) income and wealth, clearly showing that

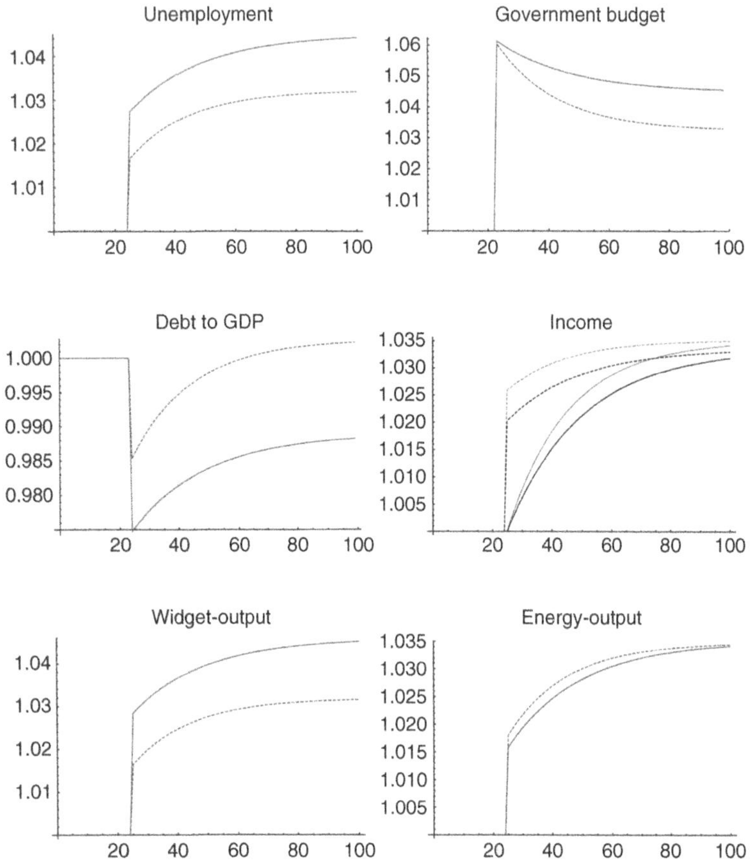

Figure 1.6 Employer of Last Resort (ELR, dashed) vs Keynesian Demand Spur (KDS, solid) policies. Unemployment decreases more and debt to GDP ratio is lower in the KDS case than in the ELR case. The budget increase is similar in both cases. Income increases for both policies and both for wage earners (gray line) and capitalists (black line). However, impacts are stronger for the ELR. The ELR implies larger energy consumption than the KDS

ELR is more efficient than KDS as a poverty alleviation policy. By directing an increase in income toward the poorest share of the population, the ELR not only alleviates unemployment but also directly improves their standard of living. What is more, this growth in income trickles down to capitalists' (dashed lines) income, making ELR a better policy for capitalists too.

Finally, ELR without its structural impacts implies a larger consumption of energy than KDS. This is due to the fact that increased income for all household sectors implies larger energy consumption by these sectors. This underlines the fact that a green job ELR implying structural energy saving is mandatory if the Kyoto Protocol has to be respected.

Two conclusions may be drawn from this analysis. First, the ELR is the fastest and most direct way to tackle unemployment and poverty. Targeting GDP or aggregate demand growth does improve the unemployment and poverty situation but is less efficient than the ELR regarding these objectives. Second, an increase in well-being for poor households implies an increase in energy either directly or indirectly through increase in widget consumption. This emphasizes the need for an energy saving policy such as the insulation part of the green job ELR.

Conclusion

Unemployment is structurally present in a capitalist economy (Keynes, 1936; Pasinetti, 1993; Ros, 2000). However, employment policies rarely target full employment (Papadimitriou, 1999; Mitchell, 2008). Usually these are "maximum employment possible under present situation" policies. We propose a job guarantee scheme that would eradicate unemployment and target lower energy consumption. Various analyses have shown that improved insulation in private and public buildings have a positive cost-benefit analysis.

The analysis done in this chapter is based on a multisectorial SFC model. This model allows us to observe output and pricing interdependencies. This is essential to show how structural changes in an industry affect other industries.

This chapter shows that a green job ELR is the best way to tackle unemployment and poverty as it is directly targeted toward these issues. The implementation of an ELR would cost less than 6 percent of public spending (leading to a 0.4 percent increase in debt to GDP ratio). This proves that sustainable full employment could be achieved, improving the situation for all household sectors.

Furthermore, this program would imply a structural change in the economy toward energy efficiency. This is essential, as the increase in income and wealth for all household sectors would imply an increase in energy use. This proves the importance of public programs in order to imply changes that would otherwise not occur. Further work would include inflation modeling and adding a more elaborate finance sector.

Acknowledgments

I would like to thank Marco Missaglia, Stephen Kinsella, Codrina Rada, and the participants of the 17th Workshop on Alternative Economic Policy in Europe for helpful conversations and comments. All errors are mine.

Notes

1. The *National Rural Employment Guarantee Act* in India and the plan *Jefes y Jefas de Hogar Desocupados* in Argentina are examples of such policies (UNCTAD, 2010; Kostzer, 2008).
2. Kaldor defined underemployment as "analogous to Keynes' definition of 'involuntary unemployment' " (Kaldor, 1968 in Ros (2000)). Ros points out that "the Kaldorian notion of underemployment is also different from [. . .] the type of unemployment analyzed by modern theories of efficiency wages" (Ros, 2000 page 96).
3. Even if full employment was attained due to an important increase in demand, it would be by working at full capacity or overfull capacity and there is a good chance that it would be highly inflationary. As Papadimitriou puts it when talking about Keynesian "pump priming" policies: "The problem is that such policies may lead to labour market tight enough to generate inflation long before 'full' employment is reached" (Papadimitriou, 1999, page a17).
4. Papadimitriou (1999) talks about a change from *Full Employment* policies toward *Maximum Employment* policies.
5. Not that the private sector is incapable of introducing technical change benefiting everyone but in some cases the cost of introducing those changes might be a barrier to these investments even if in the long run it would be profitable.
6. Sectors in this economy are thus not vertically integrated as Pasinetti (1981) defines it.
7. For a complete list of the variables, see Appendix A.
8. Haig (1921) and Simons (1938) define income as the sum of consumption and variation in wealth. According to Godley and Lavoie (2007, pp. 293–294), Haig-Simons' real disposable income comprises real disposable income minus the loss of real wealth due to inflation.
9. This has strong implications. As we will see later, firms' net wealth is positive and potentially large. This implies that depending on the propensity to consume out of wealth, there might be some cases where consumption is larger than income. At some point financial wealth might be negative. This means that capitalists borrow to consume, using their share as collateral. The value of that parameter is thus crucial (Taylor, 2008). Let's assume,

for example, that $I > S$ because investments have increased. Since I is larger than before, income increases and thus saving increases too. This increase in saving implies an increase in consumption out of wealth and thus also an increase in investments. This either stabilizes toward $I = S$ or might explode into an unstable situation. The propensity to consume out of wealth affects the accelerator.

10. In this chapter, we follow Robinson (1969) in that firms might make mistakes in their estimation of output growth creating unwanted excess capacity and Lavoie (1992) as firms also plan some excess capacity in order to avoid constraining demand in case of large growth in demand.
11. We use here a simplified version of Fazzari (1986) and Lavoie (2002), since we assume that firms have fixed targeted leverage level and return rates. The effect of these normally nonfixed variables is thus contained in γ_0. The formulation of the investment function is similar to that in Lavoie et al. (2004).
12. *Practical* or *engineer-rated* full capacity is the maximum level of production such that it allows normal maintenance and renovation of machinery to take place without impeding production (Eichner, 1976; Steindl, 1952).
13. We include capital replacement and debt servicing in the unit costs without loss of generality. The other solution would be to exclude both of these costs from unit costs and to change the dividend-related part of markup so that that part of profits can also service the debt on top of paying dividend to shareholders. Both solutions are valid. The present choice simplifies markup computation but does not allow computing the wage share easily.
14. Such a function of piecewise unit costs is based on constant marginal costs up to practical full capacity. When maintenance cannot be performed and when workers work overtime, marginal costs increase drastically implying the increasing quadratic unit costs function.
15. For more information on post-Keynesian pricing theory, see Lee (1998).
16. Appendix C contains the steady-state system of equations and the description of the steps to obtain the system.
17. Kats (2006) computes a net financial benefit of US$71 per feet of Green School built.
18. The simulations were conducted using Mathematica. The code may be found on the website http://sfc-models.net/.
19. Privately unemployed workers thus receive US$ 11 882 as unemployment subsidy before ELR is enacted and receive US$ 19 991 as ELR wage after.
20. As noted before, the total reduction or increase in employment depends on whether the energy industry is more or less labor-intensive than the widget one.
21. As seen in the previous subsection, equations (20) and (21) impede the model to reach a steady state.

References

Beveridge, W. *Full Employment in a Free Society.* New York: Norton, 1945.

Chatelain, J. The profit-investment-unemployment nexus and capacity utilization in a stock-flow consistent model. *Metroeconomica,* 61(3):454–472, 2010.

Clinch, J. P. and J. D. Healy. Cost-benefit analysis of domestic energy efficiency. *Energy Policy,* 29:113–124, 2001.

de Koning, J. Aggregate impact analysis of active labour market policy: a literature review. *International Journal of Manpower,* 22(7/8):707–735, 2001.

Dos Santos, C. H. and G. Zezza. The role of monetary policy in post-Keynesian stock-flow consistent macroeconomic growth models: preliminary results. In M. Lavoie, editor, *Central Banking in the Modern World: Alternative Perspectives.* Chetenham: Edward Elgar, 2004.

Dos Santos, C. H. and G. Zezza. Distribution and growth in a post-Keynesian stock-flow consistent model. In N Salvadori, editor, *Economic Growth and Distribution. On the Nature and Causes of the Wealth of Nations.* Cheltenham: Edward Elgar, 2006.

Dos Santos, C. H. and G. Zezza. A simplified, benchmark, stock-flow consistent post-Keynesian growth model. *Metroeconomica,* 59(3):441–478, 2008.

Dos Santos, C. H. and A. C. Macedo e Silva. Revisiting (and connecting) Marglin-Bhaduri and Minsky: an SFC look at financialization and profit-led growth. *The Levy Economics Institute of Bard College Working Paper,* 567, 2009.

Eichner, A. S. *The Megacorp and Oligopoly: Micro Foundations of Macro Dynamics.* Cambridge: Cambridge University Press, 1976.

Fazzari, S. M. and T. L. Mott. The investment theories of Kalecki and Keynes: an empirical study of firm data, 1970–1982. *Journal of Post Keynesian Economics,* 9(2):171–187, 1986–1987.

Foley, D. and L. Taylor. A heterodox growth and distribution model. In N. Salvadori, editor, *Economic Growth and Distribution. On the Nature and Causes of the Wealth of Nations.* Cheltenham: Edward Elgar, 2006.

Forstater, M. Flexible full employment: structural implications of discretionary public sector employment. *Journal of Economic Issues,* 32(2): 557–563, 1998.

Forstater, M. Unemployment. In J. E. King, editor, *The Elgar Companion to Post Keynesian Economics.* Cheltenham: Edward Elgar, 2003.

Forstater, M. Green jobs: public service employment and environmental sustainability. *Challenge,* 49(4): 58–72, 2006.

Godley, W. and M. Lavoie. *Monetary Economics: An Integrated Approach to Credit, Money, Income, Production and Wealth.* New York: Palgrave MacMillan, 2007.

Haig, R. M. The concept of income—economic and legal aspects. In *The Federal Income Tax,* pp. 1–21. New York: Columbia University Press, 1921.

Hens, H., G. Verbeeck and B. Verdonck. Impact of energy efficiency measures on the CO_2 emissions in the residential sector, a large scale analysis. *Energy and Buildings,* 33:275–281, 2001.

Kaboub, F. Employment guarantee programs: a survey of theories and policy experiences. *The Levy Economics Institute of Bard College Working Paper*, 498, 2007.

Kaldor, N. Productivity and growth in manufacturing industry: a reply. *Economica*, 35:385–391, 1968.

Kalecki, M. *Selected Essays on the Dynamics of the Capitalist Economy*. Cambridge: Cambridge University Press, 1971.

Kats, G. Greening America's schools. http://www.leed.us/ShowFile.aspx?DocumentID=2908, 2006.

Kats, G., J. Perlman and S. Jamadagni. National review of green schools: costs, benefits, and implications for Massachusetts. http://www.cap-e.com/ewebeditpro/items/O59F7707.pdf, 2005.

Keynes, J. M. *The General Theory of Employment, Interest and Money*. London: Palgrave Macmillan, 1936.

Kinsella, S., M. Greiff, and E. J. Nell. Income distribution in a stock-flow consistent model with education and technological change. *Eastern Economic Journal*, 37:134–149, 2011.

Kostzer, D. Argentina: a case study on the plan jefes y jefas de hogar desocupados, or the employment road to economic recovery. *The Levy Economics Institute of Bard College Working Paper*, 534, 2008.

Lavoie, M. *Foundations of Post-Keynesian Economic Analysis*. Aldershot, UK: Edward Elgar, 1992.

Lavoie, M. and W. Godley. Kaleckian models of growth in a coherent stock-flow monetary framework: a Kaldorian view. *Journal of Post Keynesian Economics*, 24(2):277–311, 2001–2002.

Lavoie, M., G. Rodriguez, and M. Seccareccia. Similitudes and discrepancies in post-Keynesian and Marxist theories of investment: a theoretical and empirical investigation. *International Review of Applied Economics*, 18(2):127–149, 2004.

Lee, F. S. *Post Keynesian Theory*. Cambridge: Cambridge University Press, 1998.

Lerner, A. P. *The Economics of Control: Principles of Welfare Economics*. New York: Palgrave Macmillan, 1944.

Lerner, A. P. *Economics of Employment*. New York: McGraw-Hill, 1951.

Levine, M., D. Ürge-Vorsatz, K. Blok, L. Geng, D. Harvey, S. Lang, G. Levermore, A. Mongameli Mehlwana, S. Mirasgedis, A. Novikova, J. Rilling and H. Yoshino. Residential and commercial buildings. Technical report. In Climate Change 2007: Mitigation. Contribution of Working Group III to the Fourth Assessment Report of the Intergovernmental Panel on Climate Change [B. Metz, O. R. Davidson, P. R. Bosch, R. Dave, L. A. Meyer (eds)], 2007.

Lunghini, G. *L'età del lo spreco: Disoccupazione e bisogni sociali*. Torino: Bollati Boringhieri, 1995.

Martin, J. What works among active labour market policies: evidence from OECD countries' experience. *OECD Labour Market and Socia Policy Occasional Papers*, 35, 1998. Guy Debelle and Jeff Borland (Ed.) 'Unemployment and the Australian Labour Market', Reserve Bank of Australia, pp. 276–302, 1998.

Minsky, H. P. *Stabilizing an Unstable Economy.* New Haven: Yale University press, 1986.

Mitchell, W. Why public sector jobs creation should be fashionable. *Background Paper for Decent Work Forum,* 29, 2007.

Mitchell, W. and J. Muysken. Full employment abandoned: shifting sands and policy failures. *Centre of Full Employment and Equity Working Paper*, 08-01, 2008.

OECD. OECD statextracts, 2011. URL http://stats.oecd.org

POST. Household energy efficiency, parliament office of science and technology postnote no. 249. Technical report, Parliament Office of Science and Technology, 2005.

Papadimitriou, D. P. Full employment has not been achieved. *The Levy Economics Institute of Bard College Public Policy Brief,* 53, 1999.

Pasinetti, L. *Structural Change and Economic Growth: A Theoretical Essay on the Dynamics of the Wealth of Nations.* Cambridge: Cambridge University Press, 1981.

Pasinetti, L. *Structural Economic Dynamics: A Theory of the Economic Consequences of Human Learning.* Cambridge University Press, 1993.

Passarela, M. A simplified stock-flow consistent dynamic model of the systemic financial fragility in the 'New Capitalism'. Journal of Economic Behavior & Organization 83 (3): 570–582, 2012.

Robinson, J. A further note. *The Review of Economic Studies*, 36(2):260–262, 1969.

Ros, J. *Development Theory and the Economics of Growth.* Ann Arbor: The University of Michigan Press, 2000.

Schumpeter, J. A. *The Theory of Economic Development.* Cambridge, MA: Harvard University Press, 1934/1912.

Pascal Seppecher. Flexibility of wages and macroeconomic instability in an agent-based computational model with endogenous money. Macroeconomic Dynamics, 16, pp 284–297. 2012.

Simons, H. C. *Personal Income Taxation: The Definition of Income as a Problem of Fiscal Policy.* Chicago, IL: Chicago University Press, 1938.

Steindl, J. *Maturity and Stagnation in American Capitalism.* Oxford: Basil Blackwell, 1952.

Taylor, L. A foxy hedgehog: Wynne Godley and macroeconomic modelling. *Cambridge Journal of Economics*, 32:639–663, 2008.

UNCTAD. Trade and development report. Employment, globalization and development. Technical report, United Nations Conference on Trade and Development, Geneva, 2010.

Xenergy Inc and Sera Architects. Green city buildings: applying the LEED rating system. Technical report, Portland Energy Office, June 2000.

Notations

Variable

Table 1.6 Variable definitions

YD_x	Nominal disposable income of sector x
yd_x	Real disposable income of sector x
$C_{x,y}$	Nominal consumption from sector x of good y
$c_{x,y}$	Real consumption from sector x of good y
M_x	Money deposits of household sector x
B_x	Bonds holding of household sector x
V_x	Nominal wealth of sector x
$V_{f,x}$	Financial wealth of household sector x
v_x	Real wealth of household sector x
cpi_x	Consumer price index of sector x
π_x	Inflation related to consumer price index of sector x
Y_y	Nominal output of sector y
y_y	Real output of sector y
$y_{fc,y}$	Full capacity output of sector y
u_y	Capacity utilisation rate of sector y
i_y	Real investment of sector y
$g_{k,y}$	Capital growth rate of sector y
p_y	Price of good y
F_y	Profits in sector y
RE_y	Retained earnings in sector y
UC_y	Unit cost of good y
θ_y	Profits related part of sector y mark-up
ϕ_y	Retained earnings related part of sector y mark-up
ρ_y	Borrowed share of investment of sector y
λ_y	Leverage rate of sector y
L_y	Total loans in sector y
V_y	Net wealth in sector y
N_y	Employment in sector y
L	Total loans
M	Total cash holding
B_b	Bonds held by banks
F_b	Banks profits
U	Total unemployment
G	Total public spending
T	Total taxes receipt
T_x	Taxes of sector x
B_s	Bonds supply
B_d	Bonds demand

Parameters

Table 1.7 Parameter definitions

$\alpha_{h,0}$	Autonomous consumption for wage earners	0
$\alpha_{h,1}$	Propensity to consume for wage earners based on its real disposable income	0.726
$\alpha_{h,2}$	Propensity to consume for wage earners based on its real wealth	0.07
$\alpha_{ca,0}$	Autonomous consumption for capitalists	0
$\alpha_{ca,1}$	Propensity to consume for capitalists based on its real disposable income	0.726
$\alpha_{ca,2}$	Propensity to consume for capitalists based on its real wealth	0.04
β_h	Energy consumption preference for wage earners	0.085
$c_{h,e}^{min}$	Minimum energy consumption for wage earners	0
$c_{h,w}^{min}$	Minimum widget consumption for wage earners	0
$\lambda_{h,0}$	Minimum share of wealth hold as bonds for wage earners	0.1
$\lambda_{h,1}$	Propensity to hold wealth for wage earners based on bonds interest rate	0.1
β_{ca}	Energy consumption preference for capitalists	0.085
$c_{ca,e}^{min}$	Minimum energy consumption for capitalists	0
$c_{ca,w}^{min}$	Minimum widget consumption for capitalists	0
$\lambda_{ca,0}$	Minimum share of wealth hold as bonds for capitalists	0.3
$\lambda_{ca,1}$	Propensity to hold wealth for capitalists based on bonds interest rate	0.2
θ_h	Tax rate for wage earners	0.14
θ_{ca}	Tax rate for capitalists	0.07
$pr_{n,e}$	Labor productivity in energy sector	109 355.8
$pr_{i,e}$	Capital productivity in energy sector	98.913
$pr_{n,i}$	Labor productivity in capital good sector	101 816.1
$pr_{e,i}$	Energy productivity in capital good sector	93.998
$pr_{i,i}$	Capital productivity in capital good sector	116.532
$pr_{n,w}$	Labor productivity in widget sector	82 801.08
$pr_{e,w}$	Energy productivity in widget sector	95.407
$pr_{i,w}$	Capital productivity in widget sector	106.278
γ_0	Minimum capital growth	0
γ_1	Desired increase in capital growth based on capacity utilisation rate	1
δ	Depreciation rate of capital	0.1
λ^T	Targeted leverage level	0.8
u^T	Targeted capacity utilisation rate	0.75
r_s	Return on capital	0.03
r_l	Interest rate on loans	0.04
r_b	Interest rate on bonds	0.01
G_T	Unemployment benefit	11882
W_{ELR}	ELR wage	24685
W_e	Nominal wage in energy sector	61 753
W_i	Nominal wage in capital good sector	63 481
W_w	Nominal wage in widget sector	58 722

$\overline{N}$	Total labor force	154 142 000
$C_{g,e}$	Energy consumption by public sector	7.910[9]
$C_{g,w}$	Widget consumption by public sector	6.910[11]
ξ_h	Green job impact on household energy consumption	0.1
ξ_g	Green job impact on public energy consumption	1

Appendix A: Model equations

1. Wage earners

$$YD_h = (1-\theta_h)\left[W_e N_e + W_w N_w + W_i N_i\right] + \overline{G_T} U + r_b B_{h,-1}$$

$$cpi_h = \beta_h p_e + (1-\beta_h)\, p_w$$

$$\pi_h = \frac{cpi_h - cpi_{h,-1}}{cpi_{h,-1}}$$

$$yd_h^{hs} = \frac{YD_h}{cpi_h} - \frac{\pi_h V_{h,-1}}{cpi_h}$$

$$c_h = \alpha_{h,0} + \alpha_{h,1} yd_h + \alpha_{h,2} v_{h,-1}$$

$$C_h = c_h cpi_h$$

$$c_{h,e} = c_{h,e}^{\min} + \beta_h \frac{C_h - c_{h,e}^{\min} p_e - c_{h,w}^{\min} p_w}{p_e}$$

$$c_{h,w} = c_{h,w}^{\min} + (1-\beta_h)\, \frac{C_h - c_{h,e}^{\min} p_e - c_{h,w}^{\min} p_w}{p_w}$$

$$\Delta V_h = YD_h - C_h$$

$$\frac{B_h}{V_{h,-1}} = \lambda_{h,0} + \lambda_{h,1} r_b$$

$$M_h = V_h - B_h$$

Capitalists

$$YD_h = (1-\theta_{ca})\left[F_e + F_w + F_i + F_b\right] + \overline{G_T} U + r_b B_{ca,-1}$$

$$cpi_{ca} = \beta_{ca} p_e + (1-\beta_{ca})\, p_w$$

$$\pi_{ca} = \frac{cpi_{ca} - cpi_{ca,-1}}{cpi_{ca,-1}}$$

$$yd_{ca}^{hs} = \frac{YD_{ca}}{cpi_{ca}} - \frac{\pi_{ca} V_{ca,-1}}{cpi_{ca}}$$

$$c_{ca} = \alpha_{ca,0} + \alpha_{ca,1} yd_{ca} + \alpha_{ca,2} v_{ca,-1}$$

$$C_{ca} = c_{ca} cpi_{ca}$$

$$c_{ca,e} = c^{\min}_{ca,e} + \beta_{ca} \frac{C_{ca} - c^{\min}_{ca,e} p_e - c^{\min}_{ca,w} p_w}{p_e}$$

$$c_{ca,w} = c^{\min}_{ca,w} + (1 - \beta_{ca}) \frac{C_{ca} - c^{\min}_{ca,e} p_e - c^{\min}_{ca,w} p_w}{p_w}$$

$$V_{ca} = V_{fca} + V_e + V_i + V_w$$

$$\Delta V_{fca} = YD_{ca} - C_{ca}$$

$$\frac{B_{ca}}{V_{ca,-1}} = \lambda_{ca,0} + \lambda_{ca,1} r_b$$

$$M_{ca} = V_{fca} - B_{ca}$$

Demand

$$y_e = c_{h,e} + c_{ca,e} + c_{w,e} + c_{g,e} + c_{i,e}$$

$$y_i = i_e + i_i + i_w$$

$$y_w = c_{h,w} + c_{ca,w} + c_{g,w}$$

$$c_{w,e} = \frac{y_w}{pr_{e,w}}$$

$$c_{i,e} = \frac{y_i}{pr_{e,i}}$$

Employment

$$N_e = \frac{y_e}{pr_{n,e}}$$

$$N_i = \frac{y_i}{pr_{n,i}}$$

$$N_w = \frac{y_w}{pr_{n,w}}$$

$$\overline{U} = N_e + N_i + N_w$$

Investments

$$g_{k,e} = \gamma_0 + \gamma_1 \left(u_e - u^T\right)$$

$$u_e = \frac{y_e}{y_{fc,e}}$$

$$y_{fc,e} = k_{e,-1} pr_{k,e}$$

$$i_e = \max\left[g_{k,e} + \delta, 0\right] k_{e,-1}$$

$$\Delta k_e = i_e - \delta k_{e,-1}$$

$$g_{k,i} = \gamma_0 + \gamma_1 \left(u_i - u^T\right)$$

$$u_i = \frac{y_i}{y_{fc,i}}$$

$$y_{fc,i} = k_{i,-1} pr_{k,i}$$

$$i_i = \max\left[g_{k,i} + \delta, 0\right] k_{i,-1}$$

$$\Delta k_i = i_i - \delta k_{i,-1}$$

$$g_{k,w} = \gamma_0 + \gamma_1 \left(u_w - u^T\right)$$

$$u_w = \frac{y_w}{y_{fc,w}}$$

$$y_{fc,w} = k_{w,-1} pr_{k,w}$$

$$i_w = \max\left[g_{k,w} + \delta, 0\right] k_{w,-1}$$

$$\Delta k_w = i_w - \delta k_{w,-1}$$

Costs

$$UC_e = z_{2,e} \frac{W_e N_e + r_l L_{e,-1}}{y_e} + (1 - z_{2,e})(1 - z_{3,e}) \frac{W_e N_e + r_l L_{e,-1} + \delta p_k k_{e,-1}}{y_e} + z_{3,e}\left[\beta_e + \alpha_e \left(y_e - y_{fc,e}\right)^2\right]$$

$$z_{2,e} = 1 \quad if \quad u_e < u_{\min}$$

$$z_{3,e} = 1 \quad if \quad u_e > 1$$

$$UC_i = z_{2,i} \frac{W_i N_i + c_{i,e} p_e + r_l L_{i,-1}}{y_i} + (1 - z_{2,i})(1 - z_{3,i}) \frac{W_i N_i + c_{i,e} p_e + r_l L_{i,-1} + \delta p_k k_{i,-1}}{y_i} + z_{3,i}\left[\beta_i + \alpha_i \left(y_i - y_{fc,i}\right)^2\right]$$

$$z_{2,i} = 1 \quad if \quad u_i < u_{\min}$$

$$z_{3,i} = 1 \quad if \quad u_i > 1$$

$$UC_w = z_{2,w} \frac{W_w N_w + c_{w,e} p_e + r_l L_{w,-1}}{y_w} + (1 - z_{2,w})(1 - z_{3,w}) \frac{W_w N_w + c_{w,e} p_e + r_l L_{w,-1} + \delta p_k k_{w,-1}}{y_w} + \ldots\ldots + z_{3,w}\left[\beta_w + \alpha_w \left(y_w - y_{fc,w}\right)^2\right]$$

$$z_{2,w} = 1 \quad if \quad u_w < u_{\min}$$

$$z_{3,w} = 1 \quad if \quad u_w > 1$$

Prices

$$p_e = (1 + \theta_e + \phi_e)\, UC_e$$

$$F_e = r_s p_k k_{e,-1}$$

$$\theta_e = \frac{r_s p_k k_{e,-1}}{UC\left(y_e^e\right) y_e^e}$$

$$\lambda_e = \frac{L_e}{p_k k_e}$$

$$\rho_e = \max\left[\frac{\lambda^T p_k k_{e,-1} + i_e - L_{e,-1}}{i_e}, 0\right]$$

$$RE_e^e = \varphi_e UC\left(y_e^e\right) y_e^e$$

$$\varphi_e = \frac{g_{k,e} k_{e,-1} p_k}{1 + \rho_e\left(UC\left(y_e^e\right) y_e^e\right)} + z_{1,e}\frac{L_{e,-1} - \lambda^T p_k k_{e,-1} + i_e}{UC\left(y_e^e\right) y_e^e}$$

$$z_{1,e} = 1 \quad if \quad \rho_e = 0$$

$$y_e^e = y_{e,-1}\left(1 - \hat{p}_e\right)$$

$$p_i = (1 + \theta_i + \phi_i)\, UC_i$$

$$F_i = r_s p_k k_{i,-1}$$

$$\theta_i = \frac{r_s p_k k_{i,-1}}{UC\left(y_i^e\right) y_i^e}$$

$$\lambda_i = \frac{L_i}{p_k k_i}$$

$$\rho_i = \max\left[\frac{\lambda^T p_k k_{i,-1} + i_i - L_{i,-1}}{i_i}, 0\right]$$

$$RE_i^e = \varphi_i UC\left(y_i^e\right) y_i^e$$

$$\varphi_i = \frac{g_{k,e} k_{i,-1} p_k}{1 + \rho_i\left(UC\left(y_i^e\right) y_i^e\right)} + z_{1,i}\frac{L_{i,-1} - \lambda^T p_k k_{i,-1} + i_i}{UC\left(y_i^e\right) y_i^e}$$

$$z_{1,i} = 1 \quad if \quad \rho_i = 0$$

$$y_i^e = y_{i,-1}\left(1 - \hat{p}_i\right)$$

$$p_w = (1 + \theta_w + \phi_w)\, UC_w$$

$$F_w = r_s p_k k_{w,-1}$$

$$\theta_w = \frac{r_s p_k k_{w,-1}}{UC\left(y_w^e\right) y_w^e}$$

$$\lambda_w = \frac{L_w}{p_k k_w}$$

$$\rho_w = \max\left[\frac{\lambda^T p_k k_{w,-1} + i_w - L_{w,-1}}{i_w}, 0\right]$$

$$RE_w^e = \varphi_w UC\left(y_w^e\right) y_w^e$$

$$\varphi_w = \frac{g_{k,e} k_{w,-1} p_k}{1 + \rho_w \left(UC\left(y_w^e\right) y_w^e\right)} + z_{1,w} \frac{L_{w,-1} - \lambda^T p_k k_{w,-1} + i_w}{UC\left(y_w^e\right) y_w^e}$$

$$z_{1,w} = 1 \quad if \quad \rho_w = 0$$

$$y_w^e = y_{w,-1}\left(1 - \hat{p}_w\right)$$

Finance

$$RE_e = \phi_e UC_e y_e$$

$$\Delta L_e = p_k i_e - RE_e$$

$$V_e = p_k k_e - L_e$$

$$RE_i = \phi_i UC_i y_i$$

$$\Delta L_i = p_k i_i - RE_i$$

$$V_i = p_k k_i - L_i$$

$$RE_w = \phi_w UC_w y_w$$

$$\Delta L_w = p_k i_w - RE_w$$

$$V_w = p_k k_w - L_w$$

Banking Sector

$$\Delta M = \Delta M_h + \Delta M_{ca}$$

$$\Delta L = \Delta L_e + \Delta L_i + \Delta L_w$$

$$\Delta B_b = \Delta M - \Delta L$$

$$F_b = r_l\left(L_{e,-1} + L_{i,-1} + L_{w,-1}\right) + r_b B_{b,-1}$$

Government Sector

$$T = \theta_h\left[W_e N_e + W_i N_i + W_w N_w\right] + \theta_{ca}\left[F_e + F_i + F_w + F_b\right]$$

$$G = \overline{C_{g,e}} + \overline{C_{g,w}} + \overline{G_T} U + r_b B_{s,-1}$$

$$c_{g,e} = \frac{\overline{C_{g,e}}}{p_e}$$

$$c_{g,w} = \frac{\overline{C_{g,w}}}{p_w}$$

$$\Delta B_d = \Delta B_b + \Delta B_h + \Delta B_{ca}$$

$$\Delta B_s = G - T$$

Steady State

1. System of equations

Prices

$$p_k^*\left(\delta + r_l\lambda^T + r_s\right) = p_e^* u_e^* pr_{e,i} - \frac{W_e u_e^* pr_{e,i}}{pr_{e,n}}$$

$$p_k^*\left(\delta + r_l\lambda^T + r_s\right) = p_k^* u_k^* pr_{i,i} - \frac{W_i u_i^* pr_{i,i}}{pr_{i,n}} - \frac{p_e^* u_i^* pr_{i,i}}{pr_{i,e}}$$

$$p_k^*\left(\delta + r_l\lambda^T + r_s\right) = p_w^* u_w^* pr_{w,i} - \frac{W_w u_w^* pr_{w,i}}{pr_{w,n}} - \frac{p_e^* u_w^* pr_{w,i}}{pr_{w,e}}$$

Wealth, income and consumption

$$k_i^* u_i^* pr_{i,i} = \delta\left(k_i^* + k_c^* + k_w^*\right)$$

$$k_e^* u_e^* pr_{e,i} = \frac{C_{g,e}}{p_e^*} + \frac{k_i^* u_i^* pr_{i,i}}{pr_{i,e}} + \frac{k_w^* u_w^* pr_{w,i}}{pr_{w,e}} + \frac{\beta_h}{p_e^*} YD_h^* + \frac{\beta_{ca}}{p_e^*} YD_{ca}^*$$

$$k_w^* u_w^* pr_{w,i} = \frac{C_{g,w}}{p_w^*} + \frac{1-\beta_h}{p_w^*} YD_h^* + \frac{1-\beta_{ca}}{p_w^*} YD_{ca}^*$$

$$V_h^* = \frac{1-\alpha_{h,1}}{\alpha_{h,2}} YD_h^*$$

$$M_h^* = \left(1 - \lambda_{h,0} - \lambda_{h,1} r_b\right) V_h^*$$

$$B_h^* = \left(\lambda_{h,0} + \lambda_{h,1} r_b\right) V_h^*$$

$$V_{ca}^* = V_{fca}^* + (1-\lambda)\, p_k^*\left(k_e^* + k_i^* + k_w^*\right)$$

$$B_{ca}^* = \left(\lambda_{ca,0} + \lambda_{ca,1} r_b\right) V_{fca}^*$$

$$V_{ca}^* = \frac{1-\alpha_{ca,1}}{\alpha_{ca,2}} YD_{ca}^*$$

$$M_{ca}^* = \left(1 - \lambda_{ca,0} - \lambda_{ca,1} r_b\right) V_{ca}^*$$

$$YD_{ca}^* = \left(1-\theta_{ca}\right)\left(p_k^*\left(k_e^* + k_i^* + k_w^*\right)\left(r_s + \lambda^T\left(r_l - r_b\right)\right) + r_b\left(M_h^* + M_{ca}^*\right)\right) + r_b B_{ca}^*$$

$$YD_h^*\left(1 - r_b\left(\lambda_{h,0} + r_b\lambda_{h,1}\right)\frac{1-\alpha_{h,1}}{\alpha_{h,2}}\right) = \frac{u_e^* pr_{e,i}}{pr_{e,n}} k_e^*\left(\left(1-\theta_h\right) W_e^* - \overline{G}^T\right) + \frac{u_i^* pr_{i,i}}{pr_{i,n}} k_i^*\left(\left(1-\theta_h\right) W_i^* - \overline{G}^T\right) + \ldots\ldots + \frac{u_w^* pr_{w,i}}{pr_{w,n}} k_w^*\left(\left(1-\theta_h\right) W_w^* - \overline{G}^T\right) + \overline{G}^T\overline{N}$$

Steps

a. Prices—Energy sector

$$i_e^* p_k^* = RE_e^*$$

$$i_e^* p_k^* = Y_e^* - W_e^* N_e^* - r_l L_e^* - r_s p_k^* k_e^*$$

$$i_e^* p_k^* = \left(p_e^* - \frac{W_e^*}{pr_{e,n}} \right) y_e^* - p_k^* k_e^* \left(r_l \lambda + r_s \right)$$

$$\delta k_e^* p_k^* = \left(p_e^* - \frac{W_e^*}{pr_{e,n}} \right) u^T pr_{e,i} k_e^* - p_k^* k_e^* \left(r_l \lambda + r_s \right)$$

$$\left(r_l \lambda + r_s + \delta \right) k_e^* p_k^* = p_e^* u^T pr_{e,i} - \frac{W_e^* u^T pr_{e,i}}{pr_{e,n}}$$

Prices—Capital goods sector

$$i_i^* p_k^* = RE_i^*$$

$$i_i^* p_k^* = Y_i^* - W_i^* N_i^* - r_l L_i^* - r_s p_k^* k_i^*$$

$$i_i^* p_k^* = \left(p_i^* - \frac{W_i^*}{pr_{i,n}} \right) y_i^* - p_k^* k_i^* \left(r_l \lambda + r_s \right)$$

$$\delta k_i^* p_k^* = \left(p_i^* - \frac{W_i^*}{pr_{i,n}} \right) u^T pr_{i,i} k_i^* - p_k^* k_i^* \left(r_l \lambda + r_s \right)$$

$$\left(r_l \lambda + r_s + \delta \right) k_i^* p_k^* = p_i^* u^T pr_{i,i} - \frac{W_i^* u^T pr_{i,i}}{pr_{i,n}}$$

Prices—Widget sector

$$i_w^* p_k^* = RE_w^*$$

$$i_w^* p_k^* = Y_w^* - W_w^* N_w^* - r_l L_w^* - r_s p_k^* k_w^*$$

$$i_w^* p_k^* = \left(p_w^* - \frac{W_w^*}{pr_{w,n}} \right) y_w^* - p_k^* k_w^* \left(r_l \lambda + r_s \right)$$

$$\delta k_w^* p_k^* = \left(p_w^* - \frac{W_w^*}{pr_{w,n}} \right) u^T pr_{w,i} k_w^* - p_k^* k_w^* \left(r_l \lambda + r_s \right)$$

$$\left(r_l \lambda + r_s + \delta \right) k_w^* p_k^* = p_w^* u^T pr_{w,i} - \frac{W_w^* u^T pr_{w,i}}{pr_{w,n}}$$

Wealth, income, and consumption—Wage earners

$$C_h^* = YD_h^*$$

$$YD_h^* = \frac{\alpha_{h,2}}{1 - \alpha_{h,1}} V_h^*$$

$$B_h^* = (\lambda_{h,0} + \lambda_{h,1} r_b)\, V_h^*$$

$$YD_h^* = (1-\theta_h)\left[W_e^* N_e^* + W_i^* N_i^* + W_w^* N_w^*\right] + \overline{G}^T \left(\overline{N} - N_e^* - N_i^* - N_w^*\right) + r_b B_h^*$$

$$YD_h^* = \frac{u_e^* pr_{e,i}}{pr_{e,n}} k_e^* \left((1-\theta_h)\, W_i^* - \overline{G}^T\right) + \frac{u_i^* pr_{i,i}}{pr_{i,n}} k_i^* \left((1-\theta_h)\, W_i^* - \overline{G}^T\right) + \frac{u_w^* pr_{w,i}}{pr_{w,n}} k_w^* \left((1-\theta_h)\, W_w^* - \overline{G}^T\right) + \ldots\ldots + \overline{G}^T \overline{N} + r_B (\lambda_{h,0} + \lambda_{h,1} r_b) \frac{1-\alpha_{h,1}}{\alpha_{h,2}} YD_h^*$$

$$YD_h^* \left(1 - r_b (\lambda_{h,0} + r_b \lambda_{h,1}) \frac{1-\alpha_{h,1}}{\alpha_{h,2}}\right) = \frac{u_e^* pr_{e,i}}{pr_{e,n}} k_e^* \left((1-\theta_h)\, W_e^* - \overline{G}^T\right) + \frac{u_i^* pr_{i,i}}{pr_{i,n}} k_i^* \left((1-\theta_h)\, W_i^* - \overline{G}^T\right) + \ldots \quad \ldots + \frac{u_w^* pr_{w,i}}{pr_{w,n}} k_w^* \left((1-\theta_h)\, W_w^* - \overline{G}^T\right) + \overline{G}^T \overline{N}$$

Wealth, income and consumption—Capitalists

$$C_{ca}^* = YD_{ca}^*$$

$$YD_{ca}^* = \frac{\alpha_{ca,2}}{1-\alpha_{ca,1}} V_{ca}^*$$

$$B_{ca}^* = (\lambda_{ca,0} + \lambda_{ca,1} r_b)\, V_{ca}^*$$

$$V_{ca}^* = (1-\lambda)\, p_k^* \left(k_e^* + k_i^* + k_w^*\right) V_{fca}^*$$

$$F_e^* + F_i^* + F_w^* = r_s p_k^* \left(k_e^* + k_i^* + k_w^*\right)$$

$$F_b^* = r_l \lambda p_k^* \left(k_e^* + k_i^* + k_w^*\right) + r_b B_b^*$$

$$B_b^* = M_h^* + M_{ca}^* - \lambda p_k^* \left(k_e^* + k_i^* + k_w^*\right)$$

$$M_h^* = V_h^* - B_h^*$$

$$M_{ca}^* = V_{ca}^* - B_{ca}^*$$

$$YD_{ca}^* = (1-\theta_{ca})\left[p_k^* (r_s + r_l \lambda) \left(k_e^* + k_i^* + k_w^*\right) + r_b B_b^*\right] + r_b B_{ca}^*$$

$$YD_{ca}^* = (1-\theta_{ca})\left[p_k^* (r_s + \lambda (r_l - r_b)) \left(k_e^* + k_i^* + k_w^*\right) + r_b\left(M_h^* + M_{ca}^*\right)\right] + r_b B_{ca}^*$$

CHAPTER 2

Ningxia's Ecological Immigration Program: An Embryonic Employer of Last Resort Program

Josefina Y. Li

Much of the literature regarding the Job Guarantee (JG) has been on the development of theoretical foundations for their adoption to developed and developing economies. Unfortunately, few countries have adopted this proposal with the notable exception of Argentina's *Jefes de Hogar* program (Kostzer 2008). Consequently, limited real-world data puts constraints on the further development and implementation of JG programs.

This chapter examines the Ningxia Ecological Immigration Program (NEIP). NEIP is a federal program that relocates a population from an ecologically fragile location to an area that is more conducive to settlement. The primary population targeted for the NEIP is the southern part of Ningxia Hui Autonomous Region of Northwest China. NEIP has been implemented in three phases over a nearly 30-year period from 1980s to the present. While the social, economic, and environmental problems of the region may be exclusive to China, NEIP bears some embryonic characteristics of JG green jobs programs, thus allowing for an assessment of the viability of JG programs. As such JG scholars can benefit from the experiences of NEIP, at the same time that the Chinese learn from key aspects of the JG literature.

The chapter is organized into four parts. Section "Introduction of JG and Green Jobs Programs" is devoted to a brief introduction of the key features and benefits of the JG program, especially the potential application of the JG toward the creation of green jobs to meet the increasing demand of ecological sustainability. Section "Ecological Immigration Programs in Southern Ningxia" elaborates on the three phases of the NEIP. The section details their background, original proposals of each phase, challenges that were faced, successes that have been achieved, and the policy changes of each phase over time designed to deal with the problems experienced from the earlier installments. The evolution of the NEIP is presented from its origin as the Diao Zhuang (DZ) program in 1983 to the most recent "Phase Three" NEIP development. The latter bears the most similarities to JG proposals. Section "Assessment and Analysis of Ningxia's Ecological Immigration Program" presents an assessment and analysis of NEIP by examining a survey result and by comparing and contrasting NEIP to the six principles of JG. In Section "Conclusion: Recommendations for NEIP and Lessons for JG Scholars," it is argued that NEIP can benefit greatly from becoming a true JG program, while JG scholars can learn from the real experiences of the Chinese on how to create jobs that match the specific skills of workers while being environmentally conscious.

Introduction of JG and Green Jobs Programs

One of the first scholars to put forward a proposal for a federal JG program was Hyman P. Minsky (1986). JG was presented as an alternative solution during US president Johnson's "War on Poverty," and was also written as a response to the culture of poverty literature. This historical context is particularly interesting, because the NEIP was initiated as part of China's antipoverty movement.

For Minsky, the War on Poverty should not have be an attempt to end poverty by changing people. Minsky insisted that President Johnson's plan could not alleviate poverty; rather, it could only give the existing poor a better chance, thus redistributing poverty. Minsky was convinced that the focus of any antipoverty program should be tilted toward jobs, not toward transfer payments and welfare (Minsky, 1965, 1973). Thus one of the major roles of the government is to promote stable full employment (Tymoigne, 2008, p. 9). Minsky argued that the appropriate policy would be a government employment strategy (what has today become known as the JG proposals) that takes workers as they are and provides jobs that fit their skills. The JG offers employment to those who are ready, willing, and able to work, but who have not been able to find jobs at a going wage (Wray, 2000). Through a JG program, spending is targeted directly to the unemployed. Such a policy would be to create an infinitely elastic demand for labor, which is not dependent upon the short-run or long-run expectations of businesses. Only the government can create it, since the government sector is the only sector in the economy that can divorce production from the profit motive (Minsky, 1986, p. 308). Minsky envisions creating such a program based upon the earlier programs of the New Deal era, such as the Works Progress Administration (WPA), the Civilian Conservation Corp (CCC), and the National Youth Administration (NYA). During these earlier times, these programs were viewed to be temporary to get the United States through the Great Depression. Minsky believes that these programs should operate on a permanent basis. In principle, these programs should not be means-tested, because its mandate is not to generate income for the government. Rather, the mandate is to provide income for those unemployed or marginally attached to the workforce.

Later, a number of researchers from the United States, England, and Australia took up and advanced JG proposals. Their contributions include but are not limited to advancement in state theory of money to address sovereign fiscal constraints and thus JG's affordability, the application of JG to establish Green Jobs Corp, and simulation of a JG program in today's economy. Further work included serving as advisors toward the implementation of Argentina's *Jefes de Hogar* program (see Tcherneva and Wray, 2005a; 2005b) and surveying the outcomes of its implementation. This research furthered the earlier literature on JG by Hyman Minsky (1986) as well as Phillip Harvey (1989), Wendell Gordon, and Charles Killingsworth.

Unlike other forms of fiscal stimulus, the JG is a direct job creation program that takes workers as they are while paying a living wage. By doing so, it eliminates poverty that results solely from joblessness. The JG strategy is distinct from traditional fiscal policies geared toward jump-starting private investment, where the effectiveness of private investment in combating unemployment and poverty becomes dependent upon the trickle-down effects, which take too long and are insufficient.

In contrast, the JG strategy in effect sets a floor to wage income and combines this with transfer payments[1] and equalitarian taxes; a tight labor market strategy improves the distribution of income among workers. By discontinuing the preferential treatment of capital income, it becomes possible to quickly obtain partial euthanasia of the rentier, and ease the burden of income inequality. An JG strategy is less likely to feed financial fragility than private investment-led growth. Finally, the JG program pays people to work whereas existing welfare schemes pay people not to work. Through the production of goods and services, JG employment creates more demand as well as supply, easing the inflationary pressure otherwise observed with welfare programs (Bell and Wray, 2004, Minsky 1975).

A vast literature discussing JG proposals already exists; thus there is no need to go in depth here. However, for the purpose of comparing and contrasting NEIP to a true JG proposal, it is important to know what defines an JG program. Tcherneva and Wray (2005a) summarized six basic characteristics of JG: (1) it offers an infinitely elastic demand for labor; (2) it hires off the bottom; (3) it operates as a buffer stock; (4) it pays a fixed living wage; (5) it maintains and enhances human capital; and (6) JG employees perform valuable work. This chapter adopts Tcherneva and Wray's characteristics of JG programs for assessment of NEIP presented in Section "Assessment and Analysis of Ningxia's Ecological Immigration Program."

A JG workforce that is refocused toward sustainability addresses the biophysical limitations to full employment growth as it operates with a different set of objectives than the private sector (Forstater, 2006). The problems of pollution, environmental degradation, and resource depletion are at best neglected, but oftentimes exacerbated by the private sector. A JG program can confront both problems simultaneously. The JG program can incorporate a green-collar sector to make the upfront investments that are not cost-effective for the private sector, and train workers to perform those cost-ineffective environmental services. A JG green jobs program effectively translates into higher living standards, less pollution, more cleanup, safer communities and workplaces, and rejuvenated cities and communities.

A green-collar job is not a special handicap; rather, it refocuses the existing workforce to skills and training in areas that promote environmental sustainability. The development of a sustainable economy requires, for example, commercial and residential retrofits, construction of Leadership and Energy and Environmental Design (LEED)-certified buildings, construction of rooftops and community gardens, green manufacturing, recycling, environmental cleanup, and monitoring of pollutants (Forstater, 2006, pp. 63–66).

Ecological Immigration Programs in Southern Ningxia

Background of the Region

The NEIP is a type of immigration program designed for the purpose of environmental protection and ecological reparation. It takes place in Ningxia Hui Autonomous Region, which is located in the northwestern inland of China. The particular cities and districts of Ningxia studied here include eight counties and districts that span 30,400 km^2. The area is also known as Xi Hai Gu (XHG)—the poorest place in China, known for its ecological deterioration and economic stagnation (Ningxia Regional Poverty Aid Office n.d.).

The region's permanent arid climate and landscape made up mostly of bare valleys and hills make XHG particularly susceptible to the consequences of climate change. In the past 50 years, the average temperature in XHG has risen by 2.2°C, the average annual precipitation declines 9.87 mm decennially, the 400 mm rainfall line has been pushed south by 50 km, desertification and salinization are expanding with climate change resulting in ecological fragility (H. Li, 2011).

To make matters worse, overpopulation and unsustainable agricultural practices further deteriorate and in some cases collapse the ecology in the southern mountain ranges of the Ningxia Hui Autonomous Region. Agricultural production is the primary source of income for the local population, and peasants are caught in a vicious cycle. Large-scale deforestation for agricultural and industrial purposes transforms a once rich and diverse habitat into barren arid land. Soil erosion worsens at an accelerating rate, so fertility of the land falls, which results in lower agricultural output and lower income. Unable to meet subsistence, they clear more forest for crop production, which leads to worse environment degradation and lower land productivity. The cycle translates to a decline in the region's carrying capacity to a level that is no longer capable of providing for all of its residents, thus bringing poverty upon the population. Furthermore, the worsening environmental degradation brings about geological natural disasters. Drought and sand storms frequent the area, threaten the safety of the local population, reduce the agricultural output, and deepen the magnitude of poverty.

In the 1980s, the Chinese Academy of Sciences, National Bureau of Land Management, and the Food and Agriculture Organization of the United Nations visited Ningxia for a joint investigation and concluded that the carrying capacity for the XHG region is approximately 1.3 million people. The population at that time was already 2.3 million (ibid.). Human survival in the region will be increasingly difficult if the earth continues to warm and if resources are continually exhausted. It is observed that poverty and environmental degradation are interconnected and mutually reinforcing. The solution to eliminating poverty and improving the environment was to implement an ecological immigration program, and Ningxia had to act fast.

Phase One: the DZ Model (1983–1999)

The ecological immigration program was originally a part of the Regional Antipoverty Initiative in the 1980s. The DZ program was invented to essentially move an excessive population to less fragile environments with hopes that through new resource extraction, and individual endeavor, those relocated would lift themselves out of poverty. Each immigrant is allocated one hectare of land, and one 54-m^2 house. At the same time, the immigrants were to carry out reforestation and regeneration of grassland on the previous agricultural land to qualify for compensation from the government.

The government spent RMB400 million and 18 years to establish 24 DZ bases, develop 37.3 thousand hectare irrigated land, and relocate 350,000 peasants from the mountain ranges. By 1999, the population in XHG mountain ranges had reached basic subsistence (Ningxia Regional Poverty Aid Office n.d.).

The initial DZ phase was not quite the same as the later phases in three different aspects. First, the areas that were relocated in the DZ program extended across different counties, all of which had exceeded their carrying capacity. The later NEIP phases also included ecological immigrants from geo-disaster areas affected by drought, desertification, and flood. Second, the DZ program moved out only the excessive population, and the natives participated in the program on a voluntary basis, whereas successive phases of NEIP relocated the entire village so that the forest and grassland regeneration could occur without further interference. Last and most important, the management mechanisms were different. The DZ model allowed for the mobility between the new and the original residence by keeping the immigrants' hukou[2] at their original site. However, the later ecological immigrates were managed by the relocated village, their original hukou would be canceled, and their original contracted land would be retrieved by the government (Yang, 2011).

DZ immigration was not an instant success, and it was met with many problems and difficulties. The Ningxia version of the "War on

Poverty" suffered from many of the same flaws as President Johnson's plan. The program relied too heavily on supply-side human capital investments and personal endeavors. While these qualities are beneficial to have, on the aggregate, no additional jobs are created, poverty ends up getting redistributed, and it takes a long time to develop human capital (H. P. Minsky, 1968). The program also ran into other practical issues, such as hukou management, environmental challenges confronted by the new community, and lack of funding.

The DZ policy allowed the family to move to their new location, while keeping their hukou, land, and house at their original location, which was a way to encourage locals to move, but this "traveling in between" phenomenon has two problems. One, without moving hukou, the immigrants could not properly assimilate into their relocated society. The specific legislations are vague in the treatment of immigrants whose hukou is in another region. Difficulties arise regarding the immigrants' Social Security, health care, assistance payments, insurance, voter registration, property rights, and their children's attendance at the local schools (Zhang, 2011). On the other hand, since the immigrants were allowed to retain their original land and house, immigrants could continue to work the previous farmland and/or graze the pasture, which defeats the purpose of environmental restoration. Within ten years of the initiative, some immigrants returned to their hometown, some immigrants fell back below the poverty line, and some new immigrant towns experienced high crime rates. The follow-up development in the relocated region could not be sustained (C. Wang, 2005). Two, the newly established towns had better infrastructure, but it also meant higher costs of living, such as water, electricity, and consumption goods, which put economic pressure on an already suppressed population. Many immigrants retreated to harvesting firewood for cooking, which weakened the results of reforestation.

These new communities began to face similar environmental challenges as the result of two things. First, the peasants resorted to the old way of resource extraction as an attempt to bring down their cost of living as stated above. Second, the DZ program provides an opportunity of a new life, but it did not change how the locals farm. Without the proper management of water and land resources, assimilation of knowledge of sustainable agriculture, and population control, the new towns reexperienced the environmental catastrophe that had held the population back.

Lack of funding put significant constraints on the effectiveness of the program. At the early state of the construction, many projects were able to carry out alongside large hydraulic projects. As national hydraulic projects ended, funding for complementary infrastructure was lacking, while the complexity and difficulty of the construction became increasingly clear. The progress of infrastructure construction moved slower than expected, and consequently immigrants sometimes had to move in before the construction was complete. At some new towns, the immigrants had land, but had no irrigation to work the land; they had a house, but had no electricity or water to live in it. Without properly installed sewage systems, household wastewater further polluted the area's water sources, and the immigrants ended up traveling in between their two homes (Ningxia Regional Poverty Aid Office n.d.; Wang, 2007).

The DZ program provided RMB25,000 housing credit to participants, but it also required the immigrants to raise the remaining RMB12,800 for housing construction costs. Seventy-eight percent of the agricultural families had an annual income below RMB3,000, in which 32 percent had an annual income between RMB1,000 and RMB2,000. Ninety percent of the population could not afford their portion of the housing costs, which was roughly the equivalent of five years of their entire income. At the same time, due to low levels of education, lack of collateral value, and residential mobility, it was almost impossible for immigrants to obtain a loan from financial institutions. The funding issue severely dampened the enthusiasm of the affected population, reducing the number of voluntary participants (Ma and Ma, 2011).

By 1999, despite many achievements with regard to the antipoverty measures of the Chinese government, there were still 34,120,000 people living in destitution. At the same time, the area of soil erosion in China had reached 3,670,000 km^2, which accounts for 38 percent of the land, and is increasing as 10,000 km^2 per year. The area of desertification and wasteland had reached 2,600,000 km^2, and is expanding at 2,460 km^2 per year. Massive forest clearing is still happening. Biodiversity is rapidly decreasing; degradation, desertification, and salinization of grassland worsen every year (Da, Huge and Shi, 2010). The DZ program had many flaws, and adjustments had to be made. The program was indeed followed by two successive phases to eventually become the NEIP of today.

Phase Two—How It Has Improved and Its Variety of Settlement Plans (2000–2010)

The second phase of NEIP covering the period from 2000 to 2005 signaled a huge change in the antipoverty strategy by shifting the goal from tackling poverty alone to a combination of poverty and environmental problems (Da et al., 2010). As the War on Poverty continued into the late 1990s, the Chinese government started a series of new environmental protection projects across the nation, including the windbreaker project, soil erosion prevention, desertification prevention, and the Grain-for-Green plan. In 1998, Phase Two of NEIP was initiated with the Yang Huang Irrigation Ecological Immigration project, also known as the "1236" project. The project planned to invest RMB3 billion to relocate 1 million people and open up 2 million hectares of wasteland for farming over six years. Yang Huang lies on a plane with an abundance of nutrients in the soil, making the region suitable for development and cultivation. Yang Huang was also well suited to house the immigrants as a result of substantial fiscal spending on the "Ningxia Yang Huang Irrigation Project" and the "Yang Huang Hydraulic Project" during the 1980s and the 1990s. These earlier projects provided the necessary infrastructure as well as advantageous conditions for new land development. Further, Yang Haung is positioned relatively low above sea level, guaranteeing sources for irrigation, all of which made it a desirable location for Phase Two of NEIP.

The region's "Hong Si Bao Immigration Development Zone" was the main battlefield. It admitted immigrants from seven different districts of XHG, totalling 194,000 people, forming 170 villages, and opening up 400,000 hectares of irrigated farmland. A survey study at Hong Si Bao with responses from the immigrants regarding the program is presented later as a tool for assessing the effectiveness of the program.

Around the same time, running in the background was the Great Western Development Strategy, which was designed to assist the western half of China that had lagged behind in economic development to catch up with the eastern half. The strategy focused on infrastructure with an emphasis on environmental protection. In 2001, NEIP received RMB500 million from the national government as a result of this strategy, and by 2008, Ningxia has increased its forest coverage by 819,000 hm^2 through afforestation and reforestation.

This time around, the program learned from DZ and made adjustments to deal with the three problems observed. Phase Two of NEIP adopted a population management measure that transfers the immigrant's hukou to his or her new location. This change prevented immigrants from returning to the mountains for overclearing and overgrazing on the already fragile ecosystem. It also made possible for the immigrants to acclimate to their new community, where they can enroll in the local health care and society security systems, and their children can properly register at the local school district. The new policies also considered the financial hardship of some immigrants. One of them allowed low-income families, the disabled, and the lone elderly to continue receiving welfare as in their original residence (Ningxia Regional Poverty Aid Office n.d.).

The other major problem confronting DZ immigrants was the environmental challenges they face at their new location. Without population control or changes in the fundamental farming practices, tragedy was doomed to repeat itself. Phase Two of NEIP implemented three measures to ensure ecological sustainability: ecoagriculture for water and land conservation, renewable energy sources, and reforestation.

To help the farmers make the transition to sustainable agriculture, the government provided guidance and technical support to aid the structural transformation in agricultural production, such as transitioning from subsistence crops to locally suited cash crops, setting up water-conserving mechanisms, and ecoagriculture.

For example, potato and melons are better at retaining water, thus through compensation irrigation, these produce can achieve a higher efficiency of water and land utilization and a higher yield. Xisha melon was chosen, and nicknamed "Gobi melon" by the locals for its drought resistance. With years of experimenting, the locals developed a unique way to grow this melon, which is to cover the sandy land with rocks. The shield of rocks prevents evaporation during the day, and since the arid area in Ningxia experiences great temperature difference between day and night, the cooled rocks liquefy the vapor in the air at night, watering the soil. This melon is not only tasty but also rich in minerals from the rocks and sand. The Gobi melon is a local celebratory fruit with tremendous economic benefits.

Land-conserving mechanisms such as strip cropping, alley cropping, and agroforestry, where the farmers grow trees, fruits, and vegetables in a plot of land according to certain arrangement that is mutually beneficial, and multidimensional productive mode, where crops and livestock are raised together, and waste is recycled, were adopted (Du, 2011). For example, hay may be mixed with fertilizer to grow mushrooms, and the waste from mushroom production may be used as organic fertilizer for grain production. Or in the case of growing alfalfa as forage for cattle, the waste from raising livestock can become the raw material for the biogas digester, and the organic fertilizer for crop production (Liu et al., 2011).

The second measure was the use of renewable energy. One of the reasons many immigrants in the DZ program migrated back was their inability to afford the cost of living at the new location. Oftentimes, the newly converted farmland had only received the simplest treatment, so the locals called it "raw land." One farmer had done the calculation that it takes RMB150 to "fix up" the land so it can be cultivated. Though the irrigation system, paved roads, schools, hospitals, and other infrastructure improved their standard of living, the transition from well water to tap water, from firewood to natural gas, from kerosene oil to electricity were costing far more then their previous responsibility. The RMB12,800 housing construction costs had already stripped all their savings and the costs mentioned above only aggravated their financial hardship, causing many to slide back into poverty. To ensure a smooth transition, affordable ways must be made available to provide fuel for daily activities, such as cooking, heating, showering, and so on. Multidimensional eco-agriculture practice discussed earlier provided compost fertilizer, which is a source of renewable energy. In addition, significant amount of state funding went to the distribution of solar water heaters, solar ranges, and the construction of biogas digesters and other energy-saving/emissions-reducing equipments. For example, in 2009, 70,000 solar ranges were distributed to the poor population in southern Ningxia, and it is expected to reduce carbon dioxide emission by 2–3 tons per range per year, with a sum of 140,000–200,000 tons of reduction over the lifetime of the range (H. Li, 2011). These investments were all part of the "Rural Livelihood Project"—a RMB370 billion project for the purpose of improving rural living standards in a sustainable and environmentally friendly way. The project was a component of a RMB4-trillion green stimulus package, which attempted to meet the voluntary target announced by the Chinese government at the United Nation Framework of Climate Change Conference to reduce carbon emissions per unit of GDP by 40–45 percent of the 2005 level by 2020 (IUE, CASS 2010).

The third measure taken by NEIP is afforestation and reforestation, as part of the Grain for Green, windbreaker, and desertification treatment projects. The vacated area is to be returned to forest or grassland, and the mountains closed off to grazing and farming, allowing the vegetation to recover. The second measure discussed above provided the locals renewable fuel options, which truly helped to sustain the results of reforestation. By 2009, some achievements were already visible: the forest coverage increased from 8.4 percent to 11.4 percent in Ningxia, soil erosion decreased to 53 percent, desertification came under control with droughts becoming shorter and less severe (Zhao et al. 2010). In the Grain-for-Green legislation, article No. 10 specifies that the state must provide grain or cash compensation to the participants, which amounted to 200 kg of grains, RMB20 assistance payment, and RMB50 sapling compensation annually per hectare of land returned to forest for residents in the northern provinces. The compensation may not be much, but it is crucial to the immigrants and to the society at large, because it provides incentives to perform ecological improvements. Environmental capital is a common resource, whose externalities are born by the society as a whole, but in reality few would voluntarily protect it, especially when economic benefits in forestry tend to lag behind the ecological benefits.

Although the hukou problems and the environmental challenges faced during the DZ NEIP were resolved in Phase Two, funding insufficiency persisted. As the hydraulic projects come to an end, funding directed at the immigration project also shrank. In 2004, the fund earmarked for immigration nationwide decreased from RMB1.5 billion to RMB1.2 billion, while the affected region was expanding to include nine rather than four provinces. Although Ningxia fought hard for the available funding, the amount it received was only RMB30 million, which is the equivalent of 15 percent of the amount from a year ago.

In China, the agricultural population does not own the property rights to their farmland, but it does own the long-term management rights of the farmland. If the farmer is divorced from agricultural production, the land will be annexed without any compensation. Most traditional farming populations relied on small-scale subsistence agriculture for security; thus they were reluctant to surrender land and break away from agricultural production. However, during DZ, the significant up-front costs, higher cost of living, combined with a long growing cycle generated a pessimistic outlook for the immigrants, so they responded by returning to their original residence. For new immigrants heavily burdened, the other response was to transfer the newly assigned land to those who were eager to move, thus obtaining roughly RMB20,000 to 30,000. However, the farmland and residential management rights cannot be easily transferred or are not transferable in many instances. The process of transfer is strict, long, tedious, and complicated; thus most of the sales were made privately by signing a purchasing agreement, which is not enforceable in court. Law did not protect either party in the agreements, and both parties had incentives to violate the agreement. The seller might suggest that the agreement is invalid by law, thus terminating it; the buyer might breach the agreement due to his or her inability to benefit from property rights associated with the land, which was still under the seller's name. This phenomenon could cause potential legal disputes and social unrest (L. Wang, 2009).

After transferring the land management rights, without other means of livelihood, the sellers became what Karl Marx termed "free laborers," free to work but also free from any means of production. Life was not easy for the buyers either, since their cost of moving exceeded that of the program participants, making their financial situation even harder.

The settlement plans in Phase Two of NEIP dealt with the problems that had emerged during the initial DZ phase, and they can be categorized into four broad types: collective settlement on newly converted farmland, dispersed settlement, collective settlement with land leasing, and collective settlement on a state-owned farm. The advantages and disadvantages of these settlement plans are discussed here.

Collective settlement on newly converted farmland is a form of settlement where entire villages were moved to somewhere nearby with great quantity of wasteland for conversion, whereas dispersed settlement plan placed individual households within established communities that have excessive farmland. Both plans assigned each household a house, a plot of land, or a greenhouse, and/or a milk cow or some goats. The farmland that was newly converted was usually more fertile, making it cheaper, easier, and faster to resume agricultural production while becoming accustomed to new lives (Ningxia Regional Poverty Aid Office, n.d.).

Collective settlement with land leasing was the government's response to the land transfer phenomenon. The villages were relocated to the outskirts of areas with more economic development, hence more opportunities for jobs in the manufacturing and service sectors. These jobs may pay better than working on the farms, but the immigrants may be reluctant to give up the management rights to their agricultural land. Collective settlement with land leasing allowed the population to retain the management rights of the agricultural land while freeing them to take part in the secondary or tertiary sector. At the same time, it was recognized that economies of scale also applies to agriculture. Small-scale, low-tech, dispersed production is less productive and more costly than large-scale production and management. Therefore, the government encouraged immigrants to lease unutilized land to the state, which in turn contracted them out collectively to an agricultural developer in the form of an enterprise or a cooperative, which enjoyed subsides as well as financial support from the state. Effectively, the immigrant farmer becomes a proprietor or a shareholder making rent or dividend income on his or her land, which at its very least provided for security and subsistence. The immigrant was free to either work in the nearby urban area for additional income or work on the agricultural land as a farm worker being paid a wage, which according to the policy must be higher than the Grain-for-Green assistance payment (L. Wang, 2009). Many of the previously mentioned ecoagricultural practices took place under this setting, such as growing Xisha melons, mushrooms, alfalfa, and waste recycling through compost bins and biogas digesters.

The last settlement plan implemented during Phase Two was to move the population on to state-owned farms. The property rights of the farm belonged to the state, and these farms were usually of immense size, equipped with better technology and machinery, and had the advantages that come with economies of scale production, all of which made it an ideal place for immigrant settlement (Ningxia Regional Poverty Aid Office n.d.). One example of this is the Nan Liang Farm, which is a midsize state-owned farm that occupies 60,000 hectares of land and employs 5,200 people. The farm focuses on Goji berry and corn production, and every year it requires more than 6,000 laborers to harvest the crops. Before, the farm had to hire seasonal workers from nearby towns, picking them up, paying them wages, and providing accommodations. In 2003, based on its "too much land, too few workers" situation, the farm settled 1,800 immigrants, and improved their standard of living dramatically. Every household gained access to tap water, could afford a television and a telephone, and experienced a rise in annual income from RMB500 per capita to RMB13,200–RMB26,400 per capita. It is a great leap forward from their old village in Jinyuan County of XHG, where all of the farmland came from slash and burn deforestation, grain production was terribly low, and water was so scarce that it took two hours of waiting in line to get one bucket of water from the only well in the village (Regional Poverty Aid Offce, n.d.).

During the 2000s, Phase Two of NEIP evolved to address problems that emerged during previous implementation, and most importantly the settlement model matured. While the collective settlement plan with land leasing and on a state-owned farm had achieved some success, yet two other problems surfaced.

In the 2000s, it was difficult to develop sustained follow-up industries, which are imperative for long-term development of the relocated regions and future income escalation of those relocated. Water conservation techniques, ecoagriculture, and multidimensional productions were not widespread. When left without proper guidance and training, greenhouse production output was low, the distributed cattle or goats sometimes were consumed in difficult times, and cattle grazing was unproductive and thus unpopular. Immigrants' funds were exhausted because of the initial relocation costs, the immigrant labor force was uneducated and low skilled, and thus these new communities were left with no financial or human capital to develop other industries. The two most successful collective settlement plans may have freed up individuals from the land; in reality only a few succeeded in finding jobs other than the low-skilled, low-paid manual work. It became important to develop industries near these new immigrant towns, to create and provide employment opportunities, and to train and educate this excess rural labor force for potential jobs.

Additionally, there was not enough land to host all of the approved immigrants. As the locals saw the positive results of the program, they became more enthusiastic about participating. Many residents of villages and districts asked their representatives to voice their desire to migrate and to request a raise in the immigration quota. According to the "1236" plan, 302,794 people needed to move out of the Mt. Liu Pan forest area, which was a key area of drought and desertification treatment, as well as the inundated areas, but by 2007 only 39.8 percent of the budgeted population were approved.

In short, Ningxia is short of reclaimable land, NEIP is caught in the middle of China's urbanization and agricultural mechanization movements, and the immigrants are caught in the role transformation from farmers to nonagricultural migrant rural workers. A form of settlement arrangement without land but with employment had to be developed.

Phase Three: Employment Settlement Plans (2010–present)

Phase Three as part of China's 12th five-year-plan in 2010 is another massive program. It plans to move yet another 346,000 people out of the ecologically fragile area, build 342 immigrant development zones, open up 255,000 hectares of farmland, modify 326,000 hectares, build 16,000 greenhouses, and construct 79,000 houses, all with an investment of RMB11 billion over five years. By 2015, China will have migrated cumulatively 1 million people (Du, 2011) (Zhang and Bai, 2011). In 2011 alone, the first round of construction built 81 immigration settlement bases, 32,000 household residences, and the corresponding infrastructure. In the new settlement arrangements, political and Social Security systems continue to improve and be perfected (Li et al., 2012). Emphasis has been placed on the development of advanced industrial agriculture, specialty plantations, livestock production, and nonagricultural employment. In the north Huang Guan district of Ningxia, the new plan proposes to grow

Goji berries, wine grapes, and other exotic local produce, and to develop the dairy and wool industry. The region also depends on Qian Huang industrial park to create and provide nonagricultural employment, and to train and steer the immigrants into the secondary and tertiary sectors.

Working broadly under China's 12th five-year plan, various types of employment settlement plans have become prevalent since 2011. These settlement arrangements guarantee employment for the immigrants that can take place with or without land. Each locality designs its own plan that uniquely fits its specific conditions. The settlement arrangements in Yinchuan City, Qintongxia City, and Huinong County provide notable case studies of the current "Phase Three" version of NEIP.

In Yinchuan City of Jinfeng County, the plan was known as "121," where every household was allocated one house, two hectares of a fully equipped greenhouse, or one job. The county was estimated to build two villages to settle 750 households, a total of 3,000 people. The project officially began on April 8, 2011, and by October 30, 2011, the first segment was completed to host 300 households. In addition to these, infrastructure such as the roads, schools, water systems, model greenhouses, and plant nurseries were also in place. The county government held 12 training sessions of greenhouse production to ensure that the immigrants have the proper skills and technology. To provide guaranteed positions, the county career service agency collected information from both private local enterprises and the immigrants, and tried to match available jobs in the region with skills of the immigrants. The bureau collected 1,400 positions, more than enough for every immigrant. To prepare the immigrant workers for these positions, career service agencies hosted free technical training sessions such as forklift operation, bulldozer operation, welding, and landscaping. By providing subsidies to local enterprises that provided jobs, and by offering free training to the immigrants, most of the new residents participating in the program successfully landed a job, and continued to receive on the job training as they began (Han, 2012; Tao, 2012).

It is worth nothing that many women, who were previously outside of the labor force, are being incorporated into the program to perform work such as embroidery and cross-stitching. These opportunities offer women flexible hours and proximity to the home. This is not to say that women are forced into the labor force, but that they are given the opportunity to participate. Meaningful work provides women with a sense of self-worth, builds establish self-esteem, and eliminates some of the gender inequality and andocentric culture that is still very prevalent in rural China.

Qintongxia City was assigned to settle 3,277 households and 16,500 people, and to complete 45.8 percent of the settlement in 2011. The Guangwu immigration base in Qingtongxia City will host one-third of the program using the "1+1+1+1" model, where each family is to be allocated one hectare of irrigated farmland, one residential house, one job, and one cow. Each family's small plot of land was collectively leased to Xitianlong, a sustainable wine grape production company, where the immigrants receive RMB2,000 of rent income, and a possible position close to home. Ningxia Shanglin Corporation collectively manages the cows using modern methods, and pays each immigrant a minimum of RMB2,800 annual dividend, and returns a same-age cow five years later. The immigrants, with rent income and dividend providing basic security, often sought to get a nonagricultural job for additional income. To prepare this eager workforce, training sessions are provided for free, while career services are bringing in local enterprises to offer 2,000 positions. The job matching is usually done through a tentative hiring agreement between the government and the private enterprises. The firms usually obtain policy or monetary incentives for providing jobs to the immigrants. With the previous training, many immigrants became certified bulldozer operators, welders, packers, and more, and were quickly snatched by the 13 employers (Qi, 2012). If the enterprise is state-owned, then its ability to absorb an excess labor force is not hindered by the calculation of profitability and efficiency. Furthermore, the setup with the dairy production and advanced agricultural production helps speed up the process of agricultural industrialization and urbanization of the newly established rural town.

The settlement plan in Huinong County is one step closer to a JG-type program. It was the first to provide paid training sessions. Not only were the training sessions free, the immigrants received RMB1,800 per month to learn new technologies. After graduating from the training sessions, they are directly placed at the enterprises that had previously signed the hiring agreement, and they would also receive unemployment insurance and Social Security. Three hundred and ninety-eight laborers moved to Huinong in the first round of settlement, of which 382 now have stable jobs in the industry. These immigrants came from Xiji County in XHG, where their annual income was less than RMB2,000. After settlement, the immigrants could make their previous annual income in a month, and according to national statistics, 60 percent of their income comes from nonagricultural work (Chao, 2011).

Assessment and Analysis of Ningxia's Ecological Immigration Program

It is likely that the personnel responsible for NEIP were never directly exposed to the JG literature. However, through their own trial and error from real-world experimentation of NEIP over 30 years, the local government in Ningxia has figured out a unique program that has made quite some achievements and possesses a few features of the JG program.

A Survey Study in Hong Si Bao Development Zone

The assessment of NEIP is accomplished first by citing a survey study by Liu, and then by comparing NEIP to Wray and Tcherneva's classification of JG key features.

Liu (2010) conducted beneficiary research on the social and ecological effects of the program, which included a survey study in Hong Si Bao. This particular relocation project was part of the 1999–2004 second phase of the program; and the study adopted qualitative and quantitative methods. Here, some descriptive statistics are reported of the responses from the immigrants on whether they feel that the program had a positive impact on various counts. The survey took place from March to May 2008, and collected data from a sample size of 129 households in Hong Si Bao immigration zone, and randomly selected 240 households in the entire Ningxia southern mountain range.

On a macro level, Hong Si Bao was built in the middle of a wasteland; the establishment of the community actually helped improve the ecological condition of the area. Till 2008, there were 1.3 million hectares of afforestation, 950,000 hectares of reforestation, 180,000 hectares of recovered grassland. Many windbreakers and oases prevented further desertification and soil erosion. The overall conditions of infrastructure in Hong Si Bao were better than those back in the southern mountain range, whether in terms of public transportation, mass communication, or access to water.

At first glance, most individual participants responded to the survey questions positively. When asked how they felt about their standard of living, in Hong Si Bao, 35.6 percent claimed that they were at the medium or higher level, whereas only 28 percent of people in the previous southern mountain range part of Ningxia had felt that way. Eighty-six percent of the immigrants are earning more income at Hong Si Bao than they were before, and 84 percent of them feel that the land cultivation method is different than the one they used in the south; 73 percent attribute the source of change to mechanization, 12 percent to land fertility, and 9 percent to irrigation. When asked whether they want to move back to their old villages in the mountains, 94 percent reported "no," and the reason given most frequently (83 percent) was the improvement in infrastructure, and some (5 percent) felt that Hong Si Bao was a better environment for personal economic development. The 4.1 percent of those surveyed who answered "yes" attributed the reason to higher costs of living at Hong Si Bao and thus heavier workloads. Those who still lived in the south were asked if they would volunteer to move and what they think about the NEIP. Of the 94.5 percent who were willing to move out voluntarily, 90 percent said the program was very good, and 81.5 percent of people strongly agreed with the program policies. In Hong Si Bao, 63.5 percent beneficiaries reported that their stay-behind counterparts envied them (ibid). In short, according to the beneficiaries' response, NEIP has been successful in achieving a number of goals.

Compare and Contrast to JG

The following section compares Ningxia's experience with the six basic features of an ideal JG program.

JG Offers an Infinitely Elastic Demand for Labor

Does NEIP offer an infinitely elastic demand for labor? The short answer is no. JG should offer a job to anyone who is ready, willing, and able to work, and it should have no means tests or term limits. In the case of Ningxia, the program has a sustainability aspect; thus it must consider the carrying capacity of the relocation. Furthermore, in all phases of the program, lack of funding was the only problem that persisted, which put considerable constraints on the size of the program. In fact, during the later phases, more southern Ningxia locals would have liked to participate than the program could accommodate.

However, in the job component of NEIP Phase Three, as seen in Jinfeng, Qintongxia, and Huinong, the program guarantees near-full employment. In the case of collective settlement on state-run farms, all immigrants are provided a public farm job. In the other collective settlement types, the cows, greenhouses, and goats served as initial capital investments that could provide immigrants a long-term agricultural job. In fact, oftentimes, the government helped the farmers set up their greenhouses in an environmentally friendly way, taught them ecological agricultural techniques, arguably creating sustainable green jobs for the immigrants.

In a limited sense, NEIP offers an infinitely elastic demand for labor among the immigrants. It is recognized that each nation might formulate the specifics of its program in accordance with its own situation, that is, to limit the program size to the carrying capacity of the environment, though the size of its funding commitment is a self-imposed constraint. JG literature has suggested that when a government enjoys a truly sovereign control over its national currency, it is not subjected to such a financial constraint. The central bank of China is the monopoly issuer of the RMB; it can afford to monetize government expenditure for a JG program on whatever scale it deems appropriate.

According to the state theory of money, the value of fiat money depends on the stability of the state. Throughout human history, coins were used not because of their metallic properties; rather, these coins were minted with the insignia of sovereignty (Goodhart, 1998). The reason currency is always associated with the nation is that a sovereign government defines the money of account by imposing obligations to be paid to the state and deciding what it will accept in form of payment to itself. The development and operation of a fiat currency is evident in most places in the world, where money is the outcome of political economic process. The European debt crisis proves the rule of "one nation, one currency," because when public debt is denominated in a nonsovereign currency, when the individual government fiscal responsibility is separated from an independent European Central Bank monetary role, the rule is violated.

In a modern economy like China, all government spending is financed by having the treasury issue a check—usually drawn on the central bank. When this is deposited, bank reserves go up. Hence, the initial effect of an increase of government spending is that reserves increase. Tax payments as well as bond sales are made by writing a check on a private bank account. When the check clears, the bank loses reserves, so taxation and bond sales just drain excess reserves, not finance spending. If a deficit results, that just means the public is going to end up with government money (currency or more likely checks drawn on the treasury) in the first instance, most of which will be converted to interest-earning government debt supplied mainly by the treasury. In turn, this means that the government never needs to tax or to borrow its own money in order to spend—and in fact the spending has got to come first. In any country that operates with "modern money," the government can always afford to hire unemployed labor (Wray, 2000)

The People's Bank of China introduced the renminbi in 1948, shortly following the rise of the Chinese Communist Party and the transition of the country to the People's Republic of China. The transition provided the state the political stability and power to impose taxes, which must be paid in remenbi. Like all countries with a sovereign currency, as long as it is able to enforce its own tax laws, there will always be a demand for its money. Thus, the purpose of taxation is to create demand for the government currency. Given the state theory of money, if JG policy is adopted to achieve and maintain full employment, there is nothing stopping China from monetizing fiscal spending on such a program.

A true sovereign nation should not be one that is subject to a monetary regime such as fixed exchange rates, currency boards, or monetary unions. The Chinese currency had been effectively pegged to the US dollar at the rate of RMB8.28 per dollar from 1997 until July 21, 2005, when the Chinese central bank announced the switch to a managing float regime "with reference to a basket of currencies." The announcement was billed as a major regime reform. The allowed range of fluctuation in a day was later increased from 0.3 percent to 0.5 percent in 2007. In reality, data from 1994 to 2011 suggests that the changes do give the country more independence with monetary policy and more flexibility with interest rates, although the renminbi (RMB) remains closely tied to the US dollar (Su, 2012). Hence, China is not a true sovereign nation unless it adopts a pure floating exchange regime. An exchange regime switch is not proposed at this time, as it involves detailed institutional setups and as such should not be implemented until conditions mature. Due to the scope of this chapter and the complex dynamics of exchange rate regimes, their advantages and disadvantages will not be discussed here. However, China (excluding Hong Kong and Macau) holds $3.3 trillion dollar in its foreign reserves, mostly in the form of US treasury bonds and can use these to cushion against any exchange rate speculative attacks. This cushion provides China a great degree of freedom for monetary independence as well as fiscal stimulus spending, because after all no George Soros can bring down China. For all intents and purposes, though not a true sovereign nation, China has a moderate sovereign control over its national currency. Recognizing that, the national government would be less reluctant to support financially programs such as NEIP or a true JG, thus alleviating the financial pressure on the program, allowing it to absorb more indigent populations.

Tcherneva and Wray (2005b) noted that the national government must provide the wages and benefits for the program, although this does not mean that JG must be a government-run program. In all the cases, except the state-run farm and some state-owned enterprises, all the jobs are provided, administered, and funded by private enterprises. This model is able to work in Ningxia, due to a strong labor demand from the emerging manufacturing sector in small towns and cities. After the immigrants have been trained, private enterprises can benefit from absorbing them, while helping fulfill the program. Additionally, governmental policy and monetary incentives provided to the private enterprises sweeten the deal for them even more.

However, there are several problems with this arrangement. NEIP operates mainly in the form of fiscal spending, whether in terms of infrastructure building or immigrant worker job placement. The government contracts the projects out to private enterprises, and leaves it to them for allocation. We know from Modern Money Theory (Wray, 2012), money is government-issued IOUs; it is a debt relation used to allocate resources. Corruption could occur in the bidding process, and most of the monetary gains end up in the pockets of the few, that is, the CEO of the dairy company, the contractor of the construction projects, the seed company, or the investors. Minsky called these the leading sectors (H. P. Minsky, 1965). If they are at full capacity, any fiscal stimulus will cause prices to rise without full employment. Hence, not only would this setup dilute the benefits distributed to the poor and increase income inequality, it would likely cause bottleneck inflation. Furthermore, many of the private-sector jobs guaranteed to the immigrants are existing jobs. Such an arrangement defeats the purpose of using JG to reduce unemployment, since it merely shifts jobs from one person to another, rather than creating more jobs in the aggregate. Jobs in the private sectors moreover do not automatically provide a package of benefits like those provided by the public employers, which include good healthcare, childcare, sick leave, vacation, and contributions to social security. Thus, those guaranteed jobs in NEIP are not necessarily decent jobs. In fact, according to an interview done at the Longhu in 2011, the turnover rate on the arranged positions is very high, with more than half of the immigrants having changed jobs once within the first month due to the poor quality of the job (Lan, 2011).

JG Hires Off the Bottom

Unlike the traditional Keynesian type of policy, which waits for the rising aggregate demand to trickle down to the bottom, JG is not a pump-priming program. It should be established on a permanent base, to work countercyclically as a buffer stock. These pro-investment, pro-growth policies tend to hire from the cream of the crop, stimulate the leading sectors, and create bottlenecks that cause prices to rise even before full employment. By contracting out entire projects to private businesses and leaving it up to them to determine who to hire and how much to pay, NEIP is taking the pro-growth approach in the hope that as the local businesses begin to swell, the economy begins to grow, demand would start to trickle down to the workers. However, it may never reach far enough to those at the bottom, who needed it the most. By targeting directly at the workers on the bottom, guaranteeing a decent job at a base wage, JG goes to the heart of the problem. To some degree, NEIP has done just this, hiring from the bottom, moving the indigent population out of the poorest villages, but due to the limitations and flaws in the way it is set up (as discussed in the section "JG Offers an Infinitely Elastic Demand for Labor"), the program could not harvest a 100 percent of the fruit.

JG Operates with Loose Labor Markets

With JG, labor markets are loose because there is always a pool of labor available to be hired out of JG and into private firms. Marx realizes that a reserved army of the unemployed is functional, because it keeps the wages in check in order to prevent it from cutting into profits (Marx, 1990). JG maintains such a pool of labor, keeping their skills and trainings up to date on the farms or in the factories, paying them a living wage, while performing the same function as a reserved army of labor. The immigrants in NEIP were brought out of the arid barren mountains to the edge of the emerging small urban areas, where low-skilled workers are in demand. In fact, many workers were hired away quickly by other companies that provide better working conditions or better pay; hence NEIP does operate with loose labor market.

JG Pays a Fixed Living Wage

At first glance, NEIP does not pay a fixed wage to all of its participants. However, one must realize NEIP was implemented in a decentralized manner. While the overall plan came from Ningxia Autonomous Region's government, local county governments design the specifics of the program in accordance with its political and economic situation. In the case of collective settlement with land leasing, the rent immigrants receive from the agricultural firms serves as their fixed base income. In the case of Qingtongxia City, each immigrant receives a cow from the government, which is then managed by a dairy company that pays everyone an annual dividend, which also serves as a fixed base income. The compensation for farmland conversion paid by Grain for Green is also a source of fixed base income for them. However, none of those income types is a wage; rather, they are more characteristic of a welfare scheme than remuneration for work, which defeats the purpose of JG to pay people to work and not to pay people who do not work. Also, these payments alone are too little to provide for a decent standard of living.

The case of Huinong County comes the closest to paying a fixed living wage. In a two-step process, Huinong County first provides new immigrants a paid training opportunity, where each new member of the community earns RMB1,800 a month to attend training in order to obtain a marketable skill. Then, for any trainees to be hired away by a private employer, they must be paid a premium above the NEIP training "salary," making RMB1,800 the effective minimum salary. Indeed, when the trainees in Huinong found their jobs in the private sector, they all negotiated more than RMB1,800 in base salary. These workers contribute to the production of consumption goods as well as capital goods, and their salary goes into the cost of these goods and services. Worker salary is at the bottom of prices of all kinds of commodities; thus this effective minimum salary serves as a price anchor to help stabilize prices throughout the economy. More county governments in NEIP should model their programs after Huinong and pay a fixed base salary to every immigrant in the program, whether for training or a directly created public job.

JG Maintains and Enhances Human Capital

This feature is the one that NEIP has done the best. The program provided numerous opportunities for training and technological support to the immigrants. Some training is directed at teaching useful work habits and skills, and preparing them for getting certified, as in the employment settlement plans. NEIP also brought water/land-conserving, energy-efficient, and other sustainable agricultural techniques to the immigrants, helping them to increase productivity while protecting the environment.

JG Employees Perform Valuable Work

JG workers engage in useful activities, and NEIP participants certainly provide useful and productive services, whether in their agricultural and livestock production, or on the manufacturing positions. Jinfeng, Qingtongxia, and Huinong are three successful cases where human resource allocation is optimized. The regional career service collected background information on the immigrants, and matched them to new jobs based on their experience, gender, and age. For example, women learned cross-stitching, embroidery, and making clothes, and the job allows them to work at home. Men are usually trained for work on assembling lines, or to be electricians, welders, bricklayers, and so on. Although, as stated in the section "JG Offers an Infinitely Elastic Demand for Labor", since the jobs are provided by the private sector and the productive activities they are hired to do must be profitable, public services are left undone.

Overall, NEIP displays arguably four of the six principles of JG, coming quite close to a true JG program.

Conclusion: Recommendations for NEIP and Lessons for JG Scholars

From this discussion of the six characteristics of JG programs, a detailed assessment and analysis of where NEIP and its settlement plans prevail and where they fall short in all three phases, is followed by four recommendations.

One, it would be favorable for China to slowly move toward a floating nonconvertible currency to gain true sovereignty and be able to use monetary and fiscal policy more freely. It would allow the central government to provide the necessary funding for the program to absorb infinite labor supply in the rural area in Ningxia. Presently, NEIP is instituted on a regional level, but other provinces that suffer from poverty, ecological calamity, and high unemployment can also adopt the model. Decentralized administration is actually better for reasons to be discussed later.

Following recommendation one, the Chinese government needs to realize that as a sovereign nation, NEIP is financially sustainable over the long run; thus it should offer an infinitely elastic demand for labor as a true JG would. In the absence of a solvency problem, the Chinese government should adopt functional finance principles to evaluate the effectiveness of a policy or program base on its real effects on the economy and not by its financial costs (Forstater, 1999). Functional finance does not claim that the government should spend as much money as it wants on whatever it wants without any consequences. If the economy is less than full employment, the government must expand the reserves to a level consistent with a full employment level of real output. The bottom-up approach is less likely to cause bottleneck inflation than pro-investment fiscal spending. When at full employment, the fiscal authorities should fine-tune the economy, and drain excess reserves (through both increases in taxes and bond sales) to prevent inflation. Poverty and unemployment have real consequences; thus it is important to fund NEIP to its full capacity, especially since financial constraint is nonexistent and when there is great potential for job creation. In fact, some of these jobs were already created during NEIP, but were not carried out as JG jobs. The immigration project itself involves massive construction and follow-up services, and it would make more sense to offer them to the immigrants as official public sector jobs to build their own homes. It is the author's belief that many locals were indeed involved in the new zone construction, but were hired by the private contractors as unofficial seasonal workers, which does not pay any benefits and is not sustainable.

Three, it is particularly suited for NEIP to model after proposed JG Green Jobs Corp, due to the wonderful green jobs potential coming from China's green initiative. Additionally, JG, unlike private enterprises, does not have to be profitable; rather, it targets at generating economic and social benefits. Free market solutions to environmental problems do not work very well due to the different time horizons between the short-term profit expectations of businesses and long-term time horizon needed for green projects. For example, afforestation activities are labor-intensive and "green" in nature. A typical afforestation project includes project planning, onsite clearing-up, land plowing, seedling preparation, tree planting, and postplantation management, but one of the biggest issues of Grain for Green is the difficulty to sustain the positive results through postplantation management. The afforestation compensation was important to keep the farmers out of indigence, but it did not provide a sustainable solution. Oftentimes, as discussed in Section "Ecological Immigration Programs in Southern Ningxia", the immigrants were left with no choice but to reoccupy the already converted land. According to an investigation in 2008, of all the randomly selected samples, the area of undocumented occupied converted land was as large as 233.48 hm^2, making up 0.6 percent of the total sampling size (Li and Yu, 2010). Financial difficulty also resulted in deficiency in planning, professional support, tree nursery cultivation, and insect and disease prevention; insufficient or completely absent postplantation administration left the forest with a very low survival rate (Zhao et al. 2010). Afforestation is an example of a kind of job that is financially costly, but produces long-term environmental benefits. Since government is the only sector in the economy that can divorce itself from the profit motive, it can take the initiative in this regard. The current NEIP model leaves the job creation part to the private sector. Though the immigrants are performing valuable work in the factories, many important public works, such as environmental cleanup, afforestation, civic services, are left undone.

The author recommends that in addition to paying the compensation for the original conversion, Ningxia government should provide direct public green jobs to the locals for afforestation activities, including seasonal jobs such as tree planting, sapling growth, onsite clearing up, land plowing, as well as long-term jobs in postplantation administration. The immigrants are familiar with the local landscape, and they cannot be better suited for these green jobs. With some on the job training, they can care for, treat, and maintain the young trees, and manage the forest, thus solidifying the achievements of Grain for Green. Furthermore, by integrating the local community into the management decisions, its relationship with the forest changes from a user to an active custodian. NEIP's beneficiaries should be directly paid by the government to engage in not only private-sector jobs, but also public-sector green jobs in this case. It brings me to my fourth recommendation.

Four, NEIP should hire off the bottom and become a direct job creation program as a true JG would. Instead of offering companies incentives to hire, NEIP should directly hire anyone who is willing and able to work, register them as state employees working within a private enterprise, whose wage is paid for by the government. In the case of China, if private enterprises fail to comply, the immigrants can always be placed in state-owned enterprises. It eliminates the possibility of corruption in the project bidding process and in the dark room of job positions for government subsidies and incentives exchange. Private enterprises should be involved merely in providing a platform for immigrants to perform useful, meaningful, and productive activities, not in resource allocation.

Five, as a consequence of recommendation four, if those jobs are listed as official state employees, the workers should be provided a full benefit package, including health care, social security, childcare, sick leave, and so on. The benefits and safety net will help them better acclimate to the new environment. ELR should not simply create jobs—whether it is a construction job, an agricultural job, or a green job, it should also be a safe, decent, and useful job.

Section "Ecological Immigration Programs in Southern Ningxia" teases out the details of NEIP and how it perfected itself over time during the three phases; there are definitely some lessons that can be learned by JG scholars.

Critics of JG literature may point to the difficulty for the public sector to create a variety of jobs for every program participant, and remain productive. NEIP sets a good example for JG scholars in this regard. It has been successful at placing its program participants because it first considers the realistic potential and mixed skill development of its given labor pool, and then matches that with the needs of businesses. Firms may have need for additional positions, but no money to fill them. The tentative hiring agreement is a wonderful model that takes into consideration the potential human capital needs of local businesses, and then equips the unemployed labor force with needed skill sets, who are subsequently hired according to the agreement. When the government provides wages and benefit packages for the workers, firms often gladly take the workers and put them to use, especially when they have been trained. If recommendations two and three are implemented, the skills could also be matched with public goods, such as infrastructure, resource development, and long- and short-term environmental projects. Thus, JG scholars should adopt a paid training program like the one in Huinong that is great at making the transition for the unemployed or marginalized labor force to a productive position. JG programs should also work out tentative hiring agreements between the government and the private enterprises from the community, so that jobs are directly created and funded by the government but are carried out by and integrated into the private sector.

NEIP Phases Two and Three were specified to gain the most from experience, and to realize the benefits of long-term commitments. The balance between private business, both within the government control and profit-motivated enterprise, and public programs, is not a one size fits all; and the scale and terms of government control is likely to vary from case to case. China's state-owned enterprises certainly have the advantage of being able to absorb a large number of workers and providing public goods, but placing the workers with private enterprises allows them to be disciplined and incorporated into the market economy.

NEIP demonstrated numerous other benefits that JG scholars should also recognize, but to highlight a few: (1) worker skill and productivity development leading to improved standards of living; (2) greater business enterprise and higher economic growth in output resulting from additional employment inputs; (3) registration of the great many previously marginalized rural population, moving them from the informal to the formal sector; (4) greater civic participation and social equity between the two genders and among different social classes; (5) public infrastructure and resource development, again leading to higher levels of productivity and output; (6) environmental improvement and protection, both economic and noneconomic, benefiting generations to come.

The successes NEIP has achieved validate many of the benefits that JG theory and literature suggest. Benefit 1 listed above proves that JG could indeed maintain and enhance human capital, making the labor force employable. Benefit 2 suggests that when JG hires from the bottom, its bottom-up, pro-labor rather than pro-investment approach creates more demand as well as supply, easing the inflationary pressure otherwise observed with welfare programs. Benefits 3 and 4 show that the JG policy offers the institutional vehicle for achieving many other desirable social goals. Benefits 5 and 6 demonstrate that JG workers indeed perform very valuable works for the community, be it conventional public works, profit-driven private jobs, or green jobs. NEIP provides a real-world example and experiential data for JG scholars to draw on, while having immense room for itself to improve by prescribing to other JG principles.

Notes

1. The JG strategy does not eliminate all expenditures on social programs. Even with a JG there will still be expenditures on entitlement programs for those unable to work (Wray 1998, pp. 144–145).
2. Hukou is the household registration system in China. It is a unique Chinese population management mechanism. A newborn Chinese citizen must choose to register at one of the parents' hukou. Hukou can be moved for educational or employment purposes. Some regional governments have quotas on the immigration hukou. Hukou also indicates whether the citizen is an agricultural member or a member of the urban population.

References

Chao, Junxue. *Chinese Government Public Information Online.* 2011 Dec 27. http://govinfo.nlc.gov.cn/nxfz/xxgk/hnqrmzfgzw/201201/t20120104_1282028.html?classid=439 (accessed 2012 Jun 4).

Da, Gula, Jiertu Huge, and Zhu Shi. "Analysis of the Impact of Ecological Immigration Policy." *Ecological Economy* 230, no. 10 (2010).

Du, Huiying. "Ningxia Sheng Tai Yi Min Qu Fa Zhan Nong Ye JIng Ji De Si Lu Ji Shu Cuo She Ji Zheng Ce Bao Zhao Yan Jiu." *Ningxia Journal of Agriculture and Forestry Science and Technology* 52, no. 12 (2011): 153–157,

Forstater, Mathew. "Green Jobs: Public Service Employment and Environmental Sustainability," *Challenge*, 49(4), 2006, pp. 58–72.

Forstater, Mathew. "Functional Finance and Full Employment: Lessons from Lerner for Today." *Journal of Economic Issues* 33, no. 2 (1999): 475–483.

Goodhart, Charles. "The Two Concepts of Money: Implications for the Analysis of Optimal Currency Areas." *European Journal of Political Economy* no. 14 (1998): 407–432.

Han, Yun. *workercn.cn.* 2012 26–3. http://job.workercn.cn/c/2012/03/26/120326111611065258054.html (accessed 2012).

Harvey, Philip. *Securing the Right to Employment.* Princeton, NJ: Princeton University Press, 1989. Institute for Urban and Environmental Studies (IUE), Chinese Academy of Social Sciences (CASS). *Study on Low Carbon Development and Green Employment in China.* China Official Publication, ILO Office for China and Mogolia, 2010.

Kostzer, Daniel. "Argentina: A Case Study on the Plan *Jefes y Jefas de Hogar Desocupados*, or the Employment Road to Economic Recovery." Working Paper 534, Levy Economics Institute of Bard College, 2008.

Lan, Xia (ed.). "Sheng Tai Yi Min Di Yi Xian Chang-Shi Zui Shan Shi Jian." *Xinhua Net.* 2011 Aug 30. http://www.nx.xinhuanet.com/special/2011-08/30/content_23584411.htm (accessed 2012 15–6).

Li, Huoyang. "Mian Dui Qi Hou Bian Hua, Ningxia Zai Xing Dong." *Ningxia Pictorial* (2011): Vol. 12 22–27.

Li, Yaosong, Fen Xu, and Xia Li. "Ningxia Sheng Tai Yi Min Ke Chi Xu Fa Zhan Yan Jiu." *Social Sciences in Ningxia* 170, no. 1 (Jan 2012): 29–35.

Li, Yuexiang, and Feng Yu. *Ningxia Tui Geng Huan Lin Gong Cheng Yan Jiu.* Yinchuan, Ningxia: Ningxia People's Press, 2010.

Liu, Bingru, Naiping Song, and Xinguo Yang. "Mechanism Construction on Voluntary Participation of Farmers and Community to Land Degradation Contortion at Desert Grassland Area: A Case Study in Ecological Immigration Village at the Eastern Piedmont of Mt. Helan." *Ecological Economy* 236, no. 3 (2011): 34–36.

Liu, Suansuan. *Social and Ecological Beneficial Research of the Ecologcal Relocation: The Case of Ningxia.* Mater Thesis, Department of Agricultural Economic Management, Ningxia University, Ningxia University, 2010.

Ma, Mingde and Xuejuan Ma. "Jin Rong Zhi Chi Shi JIao Xia Ningxia Pin Kun Di Qu Yi Min Ban Qian Wen Ti Yan Jiu." *Inner Mongolia Science Technology & Economy* 247, no. 21 (Nov 2011).

Marx, Karl. *Capital Vol. 1.* Penguin Classics, 1990.

Minsky, H. P. "The Role of Employment Policy." In *Poverty in America,* Margeret S. Gordon (ed.). San Francisco: Chandler Publishing Company, 1965.

Minsky, H. P. "Effects of Shifts of Aggregate Demand upon Income Distribution." *American Journal of Agricultura Economics* 50, no. 2 (1968): 328–339.

Minsky, H. P. "The Strategy of Economic Policy and Income Distribution." *Annals of the American Academy of Political and Social Science* (Sep 1973), Vol. 409: 92–101.

Minsky, H. P. "The Poverty of Economic Policy", Unpublished Paper Presentation at The Graduate Institute of Cooperative Leadership, July 14, 1975.

Minsky, H.P. *Stabilizing and Unstable Economy.* New Haven: Yale University Press, 1986.

Ningxia Regional Poverty Aid Office. *Ningxia Autonomous Region Immigration Special Topic No. 13: Theories and Applications.* http://dqs.ndrc.gov.cn/gzdt/t20070118_111959.htm (accessed 2012 Jun 15).

Ningxia Regional Poverty Aid Office. "Ningxia Autonomous Region Immigration Special Topic Series No. 11: Problems and Stategies." *State Development and Reform Commission.* http://www.sdpc.gov.cn/dqjj/fpkf/ydfpbq/t20070118_112000.htm (accessed 2012 Jun 14).

Qi, Chunmei. *Xinhua net.* 2012 Apr 17. http://www.nx.xinhuanet.com/misc/2012-04/17/content_25080118.htm (accessed 2012 Jun 16).

Regional Poverty Aid Offce. "Ningxia Autonomous Region Immigration Special Series No. 17: Industrial Support, the Hope to Lift Ecological Immigrants Out of Poverty." *State Development and Reform Commission.* http://dqs.ndrc.gov.cn/gzdt/t20070122_112595.htm (accessed 2012 Jun 15), n.d.

Su, Hua-shan. "Flexibility of China's Exchange Rate Regime and Independence of Monetary Policy—An Empirical Research Based on 1994—2011 Monthly Data." *Journal of Guizhou University of Finance and Economics* 157, no. 2 (Feb 2012): 25–31.

Tao, Lina. *Ningxia News Network.* 2012 Mar 22. http://www.nxnews.net/ds/system/2012/03/22/010312420.shtml (accessed 2012 Jun 15).

Tcherneva, Pavlina R., and L. Randall Wray. *Employer of Last Resort Program: A Case Study of Argentina's Jefes de Hogar Program.* Working Paper No. 41, Center For Full Employment and Price Stability, 2005a.

Tcherneva, Pavlina R., and L. Randall Wray. *Is Argentina's Jobs Creation Project Jefes de Hogar a True Employer of Last Resot Program?* Working Paper No. 43, Center for Full Employment and Price Stability, Center for Full Employment and Price Stability, 2005b.

Tymoigne, Eric. "Minsky and Economic Policy: 'Keynesianism' All Over Again?" Working Paper No. 547, Levy Economics Institute, 2008.

Wang, Chaoliang. *Diao Zhuang Shi YI Min Kai Fa.* Beijing: China Social Sciences Press, 2005.

Wang, Long. "Study on Transfer of Management Right of Agricultural land and the Development of Ecological Immigrants in Ningxia." *Social Sciences in Ningxia* 153, no. 2 (Mar 2009): 58–63.

Wang, Yanhong. "On Several Thought of New Countryside Construction in Ningxia Autonomous Region." *Northwest Population* 28, no. 2 (2007): 55–58.

Wray, Randall L. *The Employer of Last Resort Approach to Full Employment.* Working paper No. 9, Center for Full Employment and Price Stability, 2000.

Wray, Randall L. *Modern Money Theory: A Primer on Macroeconomics for Sovereign Monetary Systems.* New York: Palgrave Macmillan, 2012.

Yang, Shengyin. "Economic Benefit Valuation of Western Ecological Immigration: A Case Study of Ningxia Hong Si Bao Development District." *Special Zone Economy,* 10 (2011): 187–189.

Zhang, Keli, and Xinping Bai. "Jin Rong Zhi Chi Sheng Tai Yi Min Di Qu Jia Kuai Kai Fa de Si Kao." *Western Finance,* no. 8 (2011): 20–21.

Zhang, Yunjian. "Xi Bu Sheng Tai Yi Min De Xiang Guan Zheng Ce Fa Lv Yan Jiu." *Forward Position* 298, no. 20 (2011): 197–200.

Zhao, Jingqi et al. "The Measures to Consolidate the Achievement of Conversion Project in Ningxia." *Journal of Agricultural Sciences* 31, no. 2 (Jun 2010).

CHAPTER 3

Beyond Full Employment: What Argentina's *Plan Jefes* Can Teach Us about the Employer of Last Resort

Pavlina R. Tcherneva

The present chapter examines the only real-world program for direct job creation that was specifically modeled after the modern Employer of Last Resort (ELR) proposal developed in the United States (Kostzer, 2008). This is Argentina's *Plan Jefes y Jefas de Hogares* (*Jefes* or *Plan Jefes* hereafter), which was launched after the 2001 financial meltdown to deal with the devastating economic fallout. *Plan Jefes* offered a voluntary job opportunity to unemployed heads of households in a community project and was federally funded but locally administered. The program design did not conform completely to the ELR proposal, but, nevertheless, exhibited important institutional features that will be examined here. The first task is to assess whether *Plan Jefes* provided the macroeconomic stabilization effects that advocates attribute to the ELR program. The second is to evaluate how ELR programs can be designed to do more than just deal with the problems of economic instability and unemployment. Though not by design, *Plan Jefes* illustrated that public employment programs can have a transformative impact on persistent socioeconomic problems such as extreme poverty and gender disparity. Because the latter two are multidimensional problems, the ELR cannot be treated as a panacea, but should be seen instead as an important policy tool that remedies some of the most entrenched and resilient causes of poverty and gender inequality.

What Is the ELR

The ELR is a proposal for a federally funded program in which the government employs all of the jobless who are ready, willing, and able to work in a public-sector project at a base wage. The proposal stems from the post-Keynesian understanding that unemployment is a monetary phenomenon and that profit-driven capitalist economies consistently fail to produce and maintain anything close to true full employment. Keynes himself had argued that governments must do everything that is humanly possible to produce "a reduction of the unemployed to the sort of levels we are experiencing in wartime . . . that is to say, an unemployed level of less than 1 per cent unemployed" (Keynes, 1980, p. 303). This tight definition of full employment is at the heart of the ELR proposal. Calls for the government to become the Employer of Last Resort ELR were popular as early as the 1930s (Kaboub, 2007), but contemporary scholarship has formalized the proposal as follows.

1. ELR offers an infinitely elastic demand for labor

ELR is not a depression solution. There are people looking for work even in expansions and this permanent and voluntary program hires the unemployed irrespective of the phase of the business cycle (Tcherneva, 2012a). Since the federal government is the only institution that can divorce the profitability of hiring from the decision to hire, the program would eliminate unemployment by taking workers "as they are" regardless of their work experience, race, age, or gender (Minsky, 1986; Wray, 1998).

2. ELR hires off the bottom

Unemployment is eliminated by direct job creation, not by "pump priming" or by raising aggregate demand. It is a bottom-up approach to policy that offers an employment safety net to those individuals who tend to be hired last and fired first from private sector work—normally the least skilled and least educated (Tcherneva, 2012a). By contrast, pro-growth pro-investment aggregate demand policies always increase demand for the highly skilled, highly educated, and highly paid workers first (Tcherneva, 2011). Once the economy begins to recover, demand starts to trickle down to other workers, but never far enough to reach all of those who wish to work. Instead of targeting some level of investment or output growth (which may or may not produce true full employment), the ELR program goes to the heart of the problem and closes the demand gap for *labor* by guaranteeing a job at a base wage (ibid.).

3. ELR operates as a buffer stock

The key countercyclical stabilization feature is its buffer stock mechanism, where labor in the ELR program is the buffer stock that fluctuates with the cycle (Mitchell, 1998). In recessions, workers who are laid-off from the private sector find jobs in the ELR program, expanding government spending counter-cyclically. Once the economy recovers, they are hired away from the public sector into better-paying private sector jobs, reducing public expenditure.

4. ELR stabilizes wages and prices

As with any buffer stock program, ELR stabilizes the price of the buffer stock—in this case, wages at the bottom (Mosler, 1997–1998, Mitchell, 1998). An ELR worker will be hired by a private employer at a premium above the ELR wage and, thus the ELR wage becomes the effective minimum wage. Although it should not compete with wages in the private sector, some argue that it should be set at the living-wage level that establishes a minimum wage-benefit standard for the economy (Tcherneva, 2006). To the extent that wages are a cost in every producible and reproducible commodity in the economy and the ELR program stabilizes them at the bottom, the program would also help stabilize prices (Forstater, 1999a). Other price stabilization features include the countercyclical mechanism that alleviates both inflationary and deflationary pressures in the economy as a whole, as well as the program's supply side effects. In contrast to income-support programs, ELR directly increases both the demand for workers and the supply of goods and services. That supply can be directed to satisfying the very needs of the previously unemployed and poor, thereby absorbing part of the ELR wage.

5. ELR spending is always at the appropriate level

With pro-growth, pro-investment pump-priming policies, economists never know exactly how much stimulus is needed to produce genuine full employment. Producing effective demand consistent with full employment is particularly difficult with such policies because the determinants of effective demand (investment, saving, and portfolio allocation) are highly subjective and not under the direct control of policymakers (Tcherneva, 2012b). With ELR, however, government spending will be no more and no less than what is necessary to hire all who wish to work (Mitchell and Wray, 2005).

6. ELR operates with loose labor markets

The program must be flexible enough to absorb new entrants in the ELR pool but also to let them go when they find private-sector employment, without major disruptions to the public-sector projects (Forstater, 1999a). A careful program design will produce a database of such tasks that can be easily shelved when there is little demand for ELR work. But it will also permit some level of experimentation if there is an unexpected influx of workers into the ELR pool. Keynes's own view was that macroeconomic stability and full employment would be achieved by hiring the jobless directly into a long-term program for the socialization of investment, where a considerable amount of investment would be under public or semipublic auspices (Keynes, 1964 [1936]). This means that at any given time, the pool of public-sector workers would be quite large. But should unemployment unexpectedly develop, the state would play the role of "entrepreneur in chief" to provide enough employment opportunities (Keynes, 1981, p. 324). In the absence of a sizeable socialization of investment, however, the ELR program would serve essentially the same function of delivering macroeconomic stabilization and full employment through direct hiring into socially useful projects. Thus some have compared the ELR program to a universal public service employment scheme (Harvey, 2000).

7. ELR is financially sustainable over the long run in sovereign currency nations

ELR proposals are normally linked to the post-Keynesian modern money and functional finance literature, which argues that countries with freely floating nonconvertible currencies face no solvency problems or technical constraints in funding these programs in perpetuity (Mosler, 1997–1998, Wray, 1998). More than that, ELR itself can serve as a benchmark for the value of such fiat currencies (Tcherneva, 2006). Currency values are very complexly determined but they essentially reflect what one can buy with the currency. Advocates argue that the ELR hourly wage pins down a basic conversion rate between labor and the currency. In other words, a "10 dollars per hour" ELR wage, for example, anchors the currency in labor power and sets the value of the dollar to be equal to six minutes of work. If the wage were doubled, then as a benchmark (recall ELR stabilizes all wages at the bottom), one dollar will exchange for three minutes of work or will erode in value by half. So when the emitter of the currency (the government) sets the exchange rate between the currency and the labor in the countercyclical buffer stock pool, it helps stabilize the value of its currency. Freely floating nonconvertible currencies today have no equivalent anchors. Finally, ELR advocates argue that in the absence of a solvency problem, the effects of government policy must be evaluated according to the principles of functional finance, namely, by the program's real effects on the economy and not by its financial costs (Forstater, 1999b).

8. ELR maintains and enhances human capital

Unlike cash transfers, this employment safety net does not waste human potential by keeping the unemployed and poor members of society in idleness and misery. Instead, it mobilizes their manpower for the public good. Even the poorest and least educated individuals has something to contribute to their community. ELR aims to find them decent work that provides both on-the-job training and other educational opportunities that prepare them for post-ELR work.

9. ELR workers perform socially useful work

ELR supplies public goods and services that the private sector generally fails to provide. There is no shortage of needs that require attention in any community, be it poor or of relative means. The job of policymakers is to carefully assess those needs and the available resources to adequately address them, as well as to improve upon current projects and implement others that may be deemed more beneficial.

10. ELR has key preventative features over the long run

Keynes recognized early that it is one thing to maintain full employment over the long run through private and public employment schemes and an entirely different thing to eliminate unemployment once it has developed in the absence of such programs (Keynes, 1980, p. 316). In the latter case, the policy response is always too small and always too late and, without a plan for direct employment, unemployment always accelerates far too quickly. Furthermore, much greater policy intervention is needed to produce job growth through pump-priming policies, which never garner sufficient support to generate anything close to true full employment.

11. ELR is an institutional vehicle to achieve other socioeconomic goals

ELR can be used as a strategic tool for addressing pressing socioeconomic problems, beyond that of unemployment. Research on direct job creation has identified some potentially transformational effects of such programs on poor women and destitute communities, which will be discussed below (Tcherneva, 2005; Tcherneva and Wray, 2005a, 2005b, 2005c, 2005d). Other scholars have advocated that ELR take the form of a Green New Deal or a Green Jobs Corps that launches a massive environmental renewal effort and public investment in green technology (Forstater, 2004).

What is *Plan Jefes* and How Well Does It Conform to the ELR Model

Argentina was once considered the success story of neoliberal policies. Yet after a decade and a half of stagnant growth and deteriorating socioeconomic conditions, in 2001 the Argentine economy plunged in its most severe crisis in history. The unemployment rate, which had been accelerating in the years prior to the financial crisis, peaked at 21.5 percent (under the conservative methodology of measuring unemployment) by May 2002 (figure 3.1). The worsening living conditions prompted thousands of people to join peaceful protests called "cacerolazo"[1] that started in December 12, 2001, and were organized by a small merchants association. During December 14–17, 2001, Frente Nacional Contra la Pobreza (FRENAPO), or the National Front Against Poverty—a broad

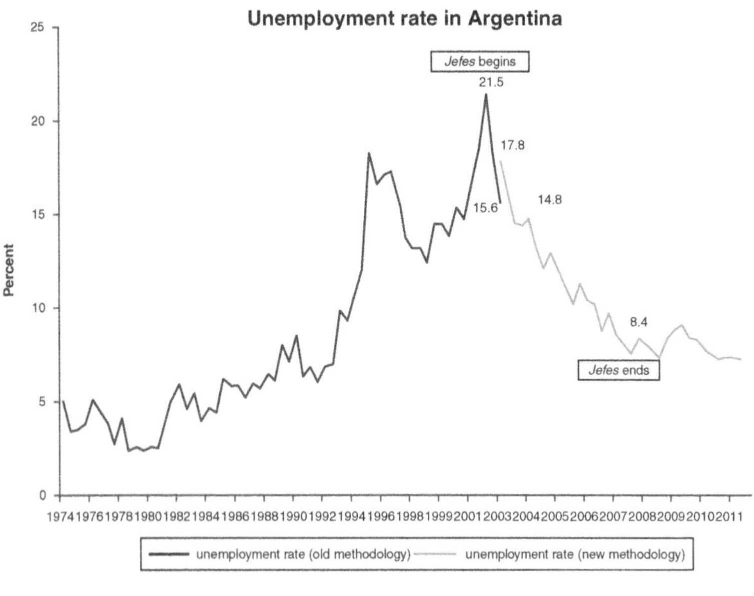

Figure 3.1 Unemployment rate in Argentina
Source: INDECH.

coalition of groups of unemployed, progressive labor, human rights, and small business organizations—organized a national campaign run exclusively by volunteers demanding the implementation of a jobs program for the unemployed from the government.

In a matter of two days protests forced both the Economic Minister Cavallo and President De la Rua out of office. The first interim president Adolfo Rodríguez Saá, who held office for only one week, signed a key presidential order establishing a job creation program for unemployed heads of households called *Plan Jefes de Hogar*. The proposal had been put together by a team of economists at the Ministry of Labor, which was modeled after the ELR proposals developed in the United States (Kostzer, 2008). The following president, Eduardo Duhale, signed the emergency decree for the establishment of *Plan Jefes* into law. It became the primary program to deal with social dislocation in the aftermath of the currency board collapse.

Plan Jefes provided a payment of 150 pesos per month to a head of household for a minimum of four hours of daily work. Participants worked primarily in community projects and were directed to training programs, including finishing basic education. To be eligible the household had to have children under age 18, persons with disabilities, or a pregnant woman. Households were generally limited to one participant in the *Jefes* program. The program's total spending peaked at 1 percent of GDP, with nearly 2 million participants. This is equivalent to about 5 percent of the population and 13 percent of the labor force.[2]

Several evaluations of the program by the Ministry of Labor (MTEySS, 2002, 2003, 2005) and the World Bank (2002, 2003) reported overwhelmingly positive results. What is of interest here is whether *Plan Jefes* performed in a manner suggested in the ELR literature.

1. Did Jefes *offer an infinitely elastic demand for labor?*

Plan Jefes was clearly implemented as a depression solution, which is how direct employment schemes are traditionally used. Although it did not provide employment to all who needed it, it, nevertheless, took workers "as they are." Jobs were provided to heads of households (presumably male), but the intrahousehold decisions in the majority of cases designated the woman as the head of the household. By 2005, nearly three-fourths of the participants who turned up for work were women (figure 3.2). There were no skills means tests and men and women were offered employment in community projects irrespective of their past labor market experience, level of education, or skill.

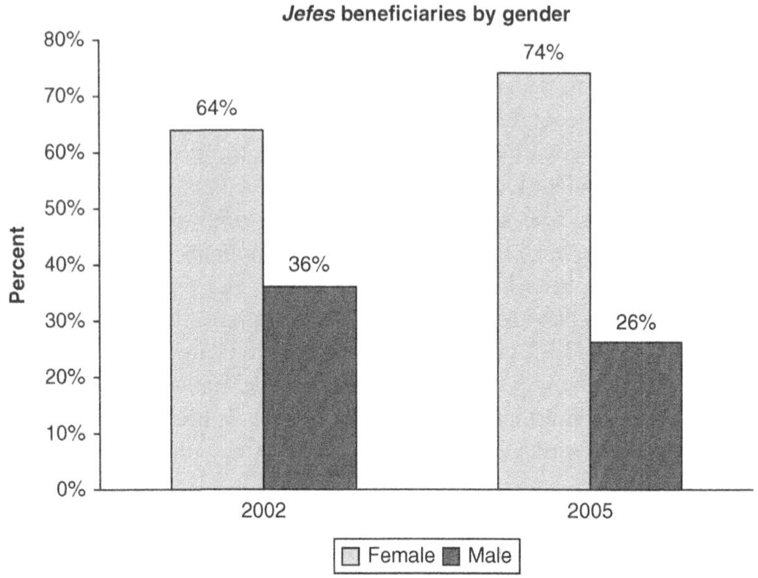

Figure 3.2 *Jefes* beneficiaries by gender
Source: Ministry of Labor, Employment and Social Security, Argentina.

2. Did Jefes *hire off the bottom?*

Data indicates that even though the program did not provide universal access to all of the unemployed the way the ELR is supposed to do, it was, nevertheless, very well targeted (MTEySS, 2002, 2003). The vast majority of program participants came from the bottom quintile of the income distribution, had high school or lower education, and experienced long spells of unemployment or precarious employment in the informal economy. Thus *Plan Jefes*, despite its primary focus on heads of households, ended up hiring from the bottom of the income distribution. Most conventional policies prime the pump to generate growth to reduce unemployment to desired levels. In the case of Argentina, the government did not wait for the economy to recover to deal with the jobless problem. Direct hiring took place before growth returned and the unemployment rate fell precipitously as the economy recovered. In other words, unemployment was not left to be a lagging indicator and growth was largely a consequence of the pro-employment strategy.

3. Did Jefes *operate as a buffer stock?*

The *Jefes* payrolls ballooned quickly. The government had estimated that only 500,000 people would show up for work, whereas at its peak *Jefes* had hired 2 million people.[3] The size of the program had prompted policymakers to devise plans to phase it out and reform it.[4] The presence of many poor and unskilled women in the program was particularly troubling to policymakers, who argued that their place was back in the home because they were largely "unemployable" (Decreto, 1506/2004). The reform was a decisive step back for women because poor women in particular benefited greatly from the access to paid community work. But while *Jefes* was still in operation, payrolls gradually and steadily shrunk in a countercyclical fashion as soon as the economy recovered. This was precisely what the ELR proposal suggests would happen. It took less than a year to see these countercyclical effects. Almost three-fourths of the male beneficiaries took up construction and manufacturing private-sector jobs, while female beneficiaries moved to the service sector. In 4.5 years, the *Jefes* payrolls fell by over 40 percent from their peak (figure 3.3). This is quite an achievement, considering that most of these workers were some of the least educated and least skilled workers in the nation. There is no way of knowing how the program would have evolved, because it was hastily reformed as soon as payrolls declined considerably. Under the new reform, the remaining men from the *Jefes* program were given traditional

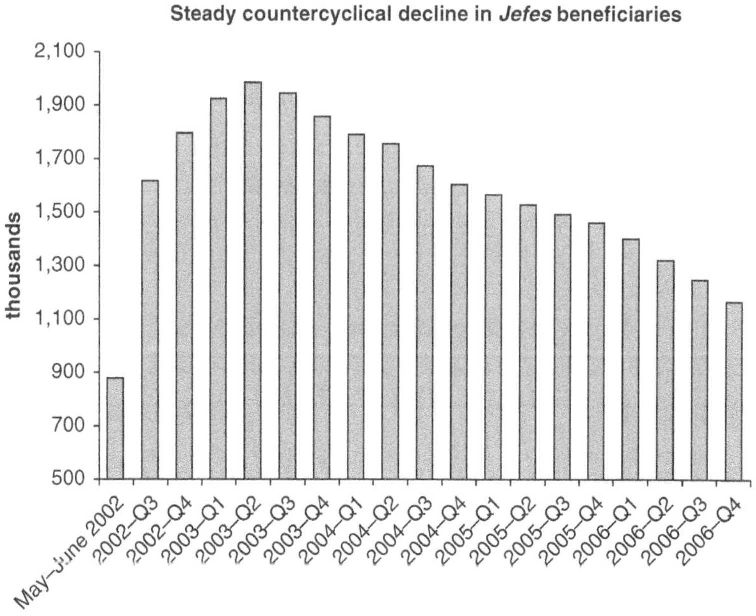

Figure 3.3 Number of *Jefes* beneficiaries over the years
Source: Ministry of Labor, Employment and Social Security, Argentina.

unemployment insurance support and were enrolled in training and education programs that would help them transition to private-sector employment. By contrast, the vast majority of *Jefes* women were moved to a conventional welfare program, which provided them with income support that varied with the number of children in the family, but which did not offer an employment opportunity (more below).

4. Did Jefes *stabilize wages and prices?*

Although Argentina's consumer and producer prices suddenly increased with the devaluation of the peso, they quickly settled down and stabilized as the economy recovered. There was some renewed price pressure during the recovery, which was largely associated with commodity price spikes and more expensive imports. Demand from *Jefes* itself, according to ministry officials, did not contribute to these pressures; indeed, these were mostly cost-push price increases. What *Jefes* did do, however, is establish a wage floor for those workers who transitioned from the *Jefes* program to private-sector work. Almost 93 percent of *Jefes* workers who were hired by private firms were offered a wage above the *Jefes* wage, which indicates that ELR-type programs stabilize the price of the buffer stock, that is, wages at the bottom (figure 3.4). It must be stressed that to be sure of these effects, one needs to study a truly universal and long-term program. Additionally the *Jefes* program helped formalize the informal sector. Beneficiaries were issued social security cards and once they moved to private employment, they were hired with traditional labor contracts that paid mandated benefits to all workers.

5. Was Jefes *spending always at the appropriate level?*

Spending depended on the number of workers who enrolled in the program and the materials necessary once the projects were approved.

The *Jefes* Wage is the Effective Minimum Wage

Distribution of beneficiaries who have been incorporated into the labor market according to salary received	
Salary received	**Percent of beneficiaries**
Less than 150 pesos	6.8%
150 – 349 pesos	30.4%
350 – 549 pesos	34.8%
550 – 749 pesos	17.7%
750 pesos and above	10.3%
TOTAL	100.0%

Figure 3.4 Wages of *Jefes* beneficiaries once they moved to private-sector employment
Source: Ministry of Labor, Employment and Social Security, Argentina.

It was "at the right level" in the sense that it was absorbed entirely by direct employment. In one other aspect, however, it was not "at the right level" because the program made no attempt to hire all who wanted to work. So while program spending was very small by most measures (less than 1 percent of GDP), considering the magnitude of the unemployment problem, it did not spend enough to hire all of the unemployed. Indeed, workers who were not eligible for *Jefes* often led protests demanding direct employment from the government as well. This led the public to increasingly associate (incorrectly) all *Jefes* beneficiaries with "violent" and "belligerent" workers, further eroding popular support for the program.

6. Did Jefes *operate with loose labor markets?*

The program was up and running in just a few months and quickly absorbed new entrants into the *Jefes* pool. It was also able to let go of *Jefes* workers once they found private-sector employment without major disruptions to public-sector projects. As indicated above, the Argentine government turned to the localities and municipalities to assess the basic needs and resources of the communities for more expedient implementation of the program. A level of experimentation clearly existed. The unemployed themselves initiated, organized, and staffed projects in their communities. While Keynes argued for the state to act as "entrepreneur in chief" (Keynes, 1981a, p. 324), in many cases in Argentina it was the poor and the unemployed themselves who showed that entrepreneurial initiative. They set up daycare centers, homeless shelters, and family attention centers for violence prevention where they were needed. The poor and their community groups petitioned the government for funding to help them set up food kitchens, subsistence farming, urban agriculture initiatives, and so on. They also organized mass recycling efforts on a scale the public sector itself had not previously done.

7. Was Jefes *financially sustainable over the long run?*

Once Argentina abandoned the currency board it had the financial freedom to employ domestic resources for the public purpose. Ability to pay in the domestic currency was no longer the problem. Though the budget was sustainable, the program itself was not expensive and it helped propel a sustainable recovery that ultimately brought the government budget into surplus.

8. Did Jefes *have key preventative features over the long run?*

As already mentioned because *Jefes* was phased out, it is not possible to assess how it would have performed as a long-term program for economic stabilization at full employment. However, in its short 4.5-year history, it became clear that *Jefes* brought key benefits to its participants. While it reduced indigency rates precipitously (by 25 percent only after five month of program operation), the decline in poverty rates was very small. This was largely due to the fact that the *Jefes* wage itself was below the poverty line. Nevertheless, poverty is a multidimensional problem and the program improved the lives of the poor in rather meaningful ways (see next section).

9. Did Jefes *maintain and enhance human capital?*

One of the most important benefits of *Plan Jefes* was that it provided an alternative to forced idleness. Beneficiary surveys indicate that for the unemployed the opportunity to earn income is not nearly as important as the opportunity to "do something" (figure 3.5). This aspect of work—to be engaged, to contribute, to participate in the community—is often overlooked when discussing the problems of unemployment. Clearly the loss of income and the inability to support oneself and one's dependents is a key problem that direct job creation programs can remedy, but they can also address many of the vile effects associated with forced idleness.

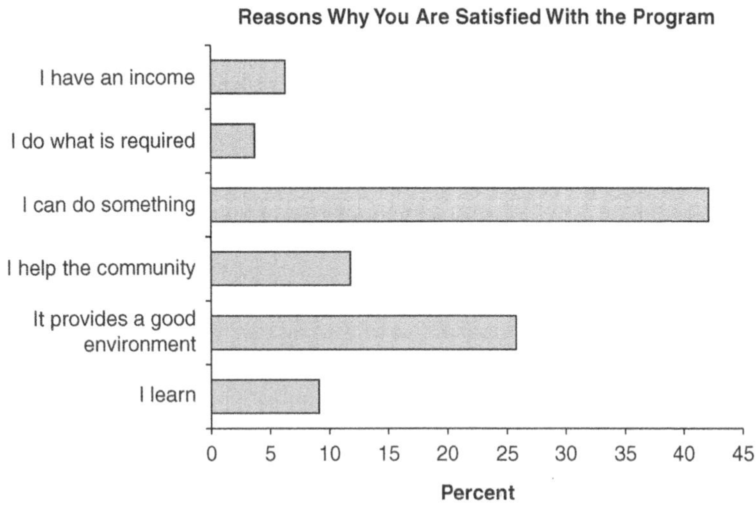

Figure 3.5 Reasons why *Jefes* beneficiaries are satisfied with the program
Source: Ministry of Labor, Employment and Social Security, Argentina.

In addition *Jefes* itself provided many supplementary programs that enhanced and improved human capital in other ways. These programs included child vaccination initiatives, health checkups, nutritional assistance, after-school activities to curb school dropout rates, and so on.

10. Did Jefes *workers perform socially useful work?*
The majority of *Jefes* projects performed useful community work. In some cases the projects literally transformed communities (more below). Projects included improvements in the water supply, sewer systems, and pluvial networks. They made investments in health and educational infrastructure, improved hydraulic defenses, clay pits, municipal slaughter houses, recreational and tourist areas, and many others. In many instances, *Jefes* funds were used as seed money by the unemployed to launch their own businesses and microenterprises, some of which made toys from recyclable materials, others manufactured clothing for the domestic or export markets, yet others set up carpentry and many other artisan shops (for details, see Tcherneva, 2005). Apart from the large-scale infrastructure initiatives, no less than 87 percent of *Jefes* projects were specifically targeted toward work in the community (MTEySS, 2002, 2003).

11. Was Jefes *an institutional vehicle to achieve other socioeconomic goals?*
The final question that requires a more detailed consideration is how to harness the potentially transformative power of the ELR program. The Argentine experience indicates that, though not by design, *Plan Jefes* delivered important and unexpected benefits to the poor and to women in particular. This is the question we turn to next.

ELR's Impact on Poverty and Gender Disparity: Lessons from *Jefes*

What the macroeconomic data reports is that *Jefes* was able, in a relatively short period of time, to exhibit some of the stabilizing features posited in the literature. Of course, without the ability to study an open-ended program that is available to all unemployed, one cannot be sure that it would perform as a genuine ELR over the long run. What is missing from the macrodata, however, is the important narrative of program participants. Although the Ministry of Labor conducted two surveys of program participants (MTEySS, 2003, 2005), survey evidence of program participants in most macrostabilization programs that deal with unemployment and poverty directly is sorely missing. Indeed, without such survey evidence, the benefits to *Jefes* workers and the communities themselves would largely remain invisible. In the case of Argentina, we have at least three separate surveys, in addition to those conducted by the Labor Ministry (ibid.) and the World Bank (2002, 2003), that I will examine here.

The work of Tcherneva (2005) and Tcherneva and Wray (2005a,b,c,d) is based on interviews of participants in several projects from two locations in Argentina—Cuidad Oculta, which was among the most destitute neighborhoods in Buenos Aires, and Almirante Brown, a downwardly mobile municipality in the outskirts of Buenos Aires. Pastoret and Tepepa's work (2006) presents narratives of poor women from *Jefes* projects in Lomas De Zamoras, a city that borders the Argentine capital. And finally, Garzon de la Roza (2006) has conducted extensive surveys of poor women from the city of Morón, also located in the Greater Buenos Aires metropolitan area.

What the surveys demonstrate is that although the official poverty rate was not considerably reduced due to the low pay of the *Jefes* program, there were other tangible ways in which the program improved the lives of the poor. Moreover, it seems that paid employment served as an empowering institution for women. Indeed, there is reason to believe that such job guarantee programs could serve as institutional vehicles that would begin to redress some of the causes of gender disparity.

Interestingly, *Jefes* was not designed to deliver the benefits that women reported in the surveys below. In fact, the program was initially called *Plan Jefes de Hogar* (i.e., program for male heads of households), and only after women enrolled in large numbers, it was renamed *Plan Jefes y Jefas de Hogar* (plan for male and female heads of household). Although not by design, it did illustrate how public employment programs can advance women's issues.

As we consider these benefits, it is worth keeping in mind that the *Jefes* program was phased out after a few years of operation and replaced by two separate programs. One of them was a conventional unemployment insurance program for men, called *Seguro de Capacitacion y Empleo,* which also assisted them with training and education and helped them transition to private-sector jobs. The other was a traditional welfare program called *Plan Familias,* which gave a cash stipend to poor women with children, but without the opportunity to work in a community project. Policymakers insisted on reforming *Jefes* on the grounds that it artificially drew women into the workforce (women who were previously inactive and did not look for work) and that the vast majority of these women were "unemployable" because they were poor, uneducated, and had many children (Decreto, 1506/2004). Those women, politicians argued, should not partake in *Jefes*, as they are already burdened by care responsibilities in the household and could not be expected to contribute to or benefit from the community project. The survey evidence that will be discussed below shows that this was not at all the case. Nevertheless, the reforms took place and were considered benevolent, because they did not require poor women with many children to work for their cash assistance, which was now provided unconditionally. Note that *Jefes* offered the opportunity to work to any head of household. It did not require poor women to work. Nevertheless, in most cases, it was the family unit that had decided to designate the woman the "head of the household" to take advantage of the job offer.

Tcherneva and Wray (2005d) report that every female participant they interviewed in *Plan Jefes* without exception wanted to work rather than receive a welfare check of equal amount. During the second evaluation of *Plan Jefes*, the Ministry of Labor also found that many women were disappointed to return to inactivity as a result of being moved into *Plan Familias* (MTEySS, 2005). A third survey by Pastoret and Tepepa (2006) found that women who moved to *Plan Familias*, but whose *Jefes* community projects were not yet discontinued, kept going back to work, even though they were now exempt from the work requirement and no longer qualified for participation in *Jefes*.

Gender Roles and Public Employment

In many public-sector projects, women tended to self-select in what are traditionally considered to be "female" work activities, but there were cases where women took on "male" jobs by setting up their own carpentry or shoe manufacturing shops, or by studying to be electricians or legal aides (Pastoret and Tepepa, 2006). While many women working in *Jefes* still defined themselves within the traditional gender roles, they also considered their work to be a form of "social motherhood" (Garzon de la Roza, 2006, 32). The primary benefit they reaped from the *Jefes* experience was a profound transformation in how they perceived their own self-worth. Their work in *Jefes* was a source of pride, which helped them acquire more power within the family. While women felt empowered from working outside the home, they did not completely escape from their gender roles within the home. Often their husbands disapproved of their employment in *Jefes,* which created conflict within the household.

However, eventually many men learned to "live with" the reality that their wives wanted to and did work outside the home (ibid., p. 117). Had the job guarantee not been there, women would have had no recourse to resist the patriarchal attitudes of their spouses.

The gender literature has often emphasized that women, who dedicate many of their resources to children and family, need to begin to enhance their own outcomes as well. *Plan Jefes* had notably allowed women to transcend the private-public divide and perceive themselves as more than just parents and domestic servants, whose sole responsibility was to raise children and maintain a household. Women reported that working and serving others was the best example they could give to their children and that they obtained many more valuable rewards from this experience than the monetary aspect, which was, nevertheless, very important to them. Women felt like they had "grown wings" (Garzon de la Roza, 2006, 87).

The involvement in community work increased solidarity and transformed neighborhoods. Garzon de la Roza (2006) reports that residents found the district of Moron to have markedly changed during the five years of *Jefes* existence. This is consistent with Tcherneva and Wray's (2005d) and Pastoret and Tepepa's (2006) findings of the transformative effects of *Jefes* projects on one of the most destitute regions of Buenos Aires: a region that was known for many years as Cuidad Oculta (the Hidden City) and that after four years of *Jefes* operation was renamed to Villa 15, as residents no longer believed to be outside the reach of public policy.

How the ELR Delivers Benefits to All but Especially to the Poor

From the experience of poor women in the *Jefes* program it seems plausible that an ELR program that is as well targeted as *Jefes* would deliver the greatest benefits to those who are truly at the bottom of the socioeconomic ladder. For example, Tcherneva (2005) reports that the beneficiaries' attitudes toward their *Jefes* experience depends in part on their level of education and previous work experience. Those men and women with higher level of education and skill and previous work experience in the formal economy appreciated the opportunity to be engaged in some community service, but did not consider *Jefes* to be "real work" and were eager to return to their private-sector jobs.

Consistent with Tcherneva and Wray's (2005d) findings, Garzon de la Roza (2006) reports that some of the better-educated individuals and those with previous work experience did not consider *Jefes* to be "real work," but that the poor and least educated women felt that *Jefes* had given them essential experience and benefits. Nonetheless, all participants agreed that only paid work enhanced dignity and that receiving traditional income/welfare support brought a certain humiliation to the recipient. Because of the importance of work, all of the interviewed *Jefes* beneficiaries felt that all social assistance needed to be "earned with work" (Garzon de la Roza, 2006, 111).

Plan Jefes was able to address not only the material but also the emotional destitution of people who had been trapped in forced inactivity for too long (ibid.). Emotional benefits were derived when women found "coherency" and "completeness" in their life, when their existing knowledge was no longer "archived" in their memory but used to help the communities, when they could escape from demeaning informal sector domestic work and create a "home away from home" in the community center (ibid., p. 104).

It was the poorest women who found empowerment and benefited the most from *Jefes*. Nonetheless, the major obstacles to their participation in the program were not their childcare responsibilities or poverty, but the social mores of policymakers regarding what was considered "productive" and "unproductive" work and who should be regarded as "employable" and "unemployable." These were the attitudes that drove the *Jefes* reform.

A Note on Program Reform: Why Paid Work Is Superior to Welfare

As noted above, in cases where *Jefes* projects were still operating, women continued to go to their places of work, but the government's effort to "encourage" them to leave *Jefes* was significant. This "marketing strategy" was partly motivated by the results of two pilot efforts to transfer *Jefes* workers to *Plan Familias*—one of the pilot programs was launched in the district of Ituzaingó, Bs.As., and the other in Santa Fé. The IADB argued that these pilot programs performed "acceptably" (IADB, 2005, 29). In Ituzaingó 94 percent of the population that was considered unemployable was successfully persuaded to transfer to *Plan Familias*, but in Santa Fe less than 50 percent of the eligible population chose to leave *Jefes* (ibid.). Because of these pilot results, it was recommended that the government expand its public relations efforts to explain the intended benefits of *Familias* to women participating in *Jefes*. In sum, paternalistic policies that presume to know what is better for the poor than the poor themselves drove the reform of *Jefes*, propelled by gender stereotypes about what type of work is productive and unproductive and which individuals are employable and unemployable.

While *Plan Familias* tried to supplement the cash transfer with various training, education, and empowerment workshops, women did not benefit from them as much as they did by having access to these through the *Jefes* program (which admittedly had too small a training and education component relative to needs). Nevertheless, the evidence indicates that poor women want to work and feel empowered from working in and for the community. An educational workshop may be able to teach them about their civil, social, and political rights, but *Jefes* allowed them to exercise them. Women can learn about empowerment in the classroom or they can be given tangible opportunities that empower. Workshops for violence prevention and information about shelters for the abused are all desirable and much needed, but *Jefes* had already begun to offer them. Furthermore, by actively participating in the provisioning of these services, women became not only "patients" of violence prevention, but "agents" of change. With *Jefes*, the burden of unpaid work associated with child rearing was not only reduced, but care was also explicitly recognized as a function of the *larger community* and not strictly of the individual family unit. This important aspect of the socialization of care has helped foster a stakeholder society and participatory democracy though public service.

The stipulation that only women are eligible for *Plan Familias* further reinforced the conservative view that women's work in *Jefes* was generally unproductive. The reform therefore called for sending them back to the home with a welfare check, providing them with information about remedial courses and training, but without the guarantee of a job available to them should they want one. This reform was essentially based on the old ideology that government policies must induce or nudge women to change their own behavior and character to become "employable" if they wanted private-sector work. Women's roles as mothers and spouses were reinforced by this reform, while at the same time attempts were made to help their husbands to transition to private-sector employment.

Poor Women Want Pay not Handouts

Poor mothers want to participate in mainstream society, to receive wages, and to contribute to private market and community production. At the same time, poor mothers feel the pressing need for mainstream society to recognize their care work and community work as useful. Women also understand that income alone does not empower. Social mores dictate that genuine empowerment comes from *earned* income, not charitable contributions. Although nonwage income entitlements to women attempt to recognize household work as socially useful work deserving of financial support in a monetized society, they do not carry the same benefits women report from engaging in paid employment, nor do they help break the gender stereotypes of division of responsibilities within the household.

Public employment safety nets such as the ELR are institutions that put human needs first as they redefine "efficient" from what is "profitable" to what is "useful" (see also Archer, 2003, on this distinction). They engage their participants directly in the goal of advancing the public purpose and are therefore programs that promote inclusion. Thus when designing fiscal policy the *inclusion/exclusion nexus* matters.

Policymakers' claim that it is undesirable to activate women through these job guarantee programs (by "artificially" bringing them into the labor market) failed to consider what poor women actually want. Women often serve as a buffer to complement the earning strategies of families during times of crisis. In terms of the power relationships within the household, women may be able do so because, during crises, their husbands may allow them to participate in work outside the home, but when family earnings are adequate, women are thrust into inactivity by social mores, their husband's attitudes, or simple lack of employment opportunities. The job guarantee by contrast recognizes the right of *all* men and women to participate in a universal employment program that redefines civic society. Men's resistance to women's participation may be less if the job guarantee is accessible to all, but, furthermore, the very existence of a guaranteed employment opportunity would provide the teeth in women's bite when they demand work outside of the home. Again it is important to note that the job guarantee and the ELR are not coercive programs; they offer income and the opportunity to work. Homemakers who prefer to stay at home will feel no obligation to join such a program and can enjoy the benefits of the universal child allowance that supplements the public employment strategy.

Why Is It Important for the ELR to Offer Access to All

The job guarantee must be a universal program, even if it can deliver key benefits especially to women. If it is not universal it will create social antagonism and reactionary sentiment, as demonstrated by the *Jefes* experience. If *Jefes* were designed as a universal program, it would have likely produced more equitable distribution between male and female participants in the program. Additionally, because *Jefes* was not universal, unemployment in Argentina was not wiped out even though it declined immediately and considerably.

If equal access was granted to all, women would have likely suffered less stigmatization than they did. Individuals who participate in public employment would not be stigmatized as much as those receiving welfare. Although it must be noted that because welfare recipients are often largely invisible, society does not always rally opposition to welfare programs, even if they are more expensive or less effective than public employment schemes. Thus it is important that the visible public output produced by women and men is both useful and needed, but is also adequately acknowledged as such.

A universal *Jefes* would have also produced a faster formalization of informal activity and a stronger countercyclical effect. Nevertheless, men still entered private-sector employment in larger numbers than did women (MTEySS, 2005),[5] indicating various barriers to entry into private-sector jobs (discrimination, lack of prior opportunities, or employment experience) or simple self-selection, if women preferred the proximity to the home. Thus the job guarantee must be accompanied with fair hiring laws, affirmative action, and other provisions. The job guarantee cannot correct all discrimination in hiring practices, but it could potentially ensure that private employers, hiring from the public-sector pool, do so on the basis of skill and not gender. Furthermore, the job guarantee itself can be designed in a way to increase the "employability" of women, but because it guarantees a job opportunity in the public sector, it also allows women to refuse private-sector employment in subpar conditions.

Finally, in *Jefes* the products and earnings from public employment were not controlled by men. Women produced, distributed, and sold their own output. They kept portions of their earnings to reinvest in the cooperatives or microenterprises, or to spend on household and children's needs. While women clearly believed themselves to be empowered by the job opportunity, it is quite possible that such empowerment may emasculate their spouses, engendering resentment toward working in the public sector. This is why universalization and not elimination of the *Jefes Plan* would have been a better course of action. Men have less resistance to female employment when both genders have access to the same opportunity, even if men do not end up taking proportionate advantage of these opportunities. In the modern context, it is less likely to improve the employment practices of multinational corporations sufficiently quickly to allow women equal employment opportunities. Although such a goal is of utmost importance, for more egalitarian labor market conditions, one step toward achieving it is by providing employment opportunities to men and women in the public sector. So long as these public-sector jobs have a gender-informed design, they will be able to incorporate the care economy in the public sphere and help redefine the meaning of work away from strict market utility toward social usefulness. Such a reconceptualization of work and of the public-sector domain is necessary for implementing sustainable and gender-aware long-term policies for macroeconomic stabilization, full employment, and poverty alleviation.

Conclusion

The literature on ELR tends to emphasize the important macroeconomic stabilization effects of the program. Importantly, this is among the very few policy proposals that secure and maintain as close an approximation to full employment as is practical over the long run. The latter objectives are after all the *raison d'être* for fiscal policy as articulated by John Maynard Keynes. As we examine the merits of the ELR proposal, there is reason to believe that the program can address concerns beyond those of unemployment. Indeed, ELR can be a transformative policy tool that deals with pressing socioeconomic problems such as poverty and gender disparity. ELR becomes not just a policy for full employment but an institution for change.

Notes

1. A form of protest where people take to the streets banging pots and pans, or "cacerolas."
2. For details on the history of the program, see Kostzer (2008).
3. This is an indication that open-ended job offers as these will bring many previously discouraged individuals back into the labor force. Thus any program design must account for the reactivation of those individuals who the official statistics fail to capture as unemployed.
4. And indeed after about 4.5 years of operation, *Jefes* was gradually closed down.
5. Although women comprised about 74 percent of *Jefes* participants in 2005, only 34 percent of all *Jefes* who found private-sector employment after enrolling in the program were women (MTEySS, 2005).

References

Decreto n° 1506/2004: http://www.desarrollosocial.gov.ar/Planes/PF/dec_1506_04.pdf, accessed May 1, 2007.

Forstater, M. 1999a. "Full Employment and Economic Flexibility." *Economic and Labour Relations Review,* 11 (Supplement): 69–88.

Forstater, M. 1999b. "Functional Finance and Full Employment: Lessons from Lerner for Today." *Journal of Economic Issues,* 33 (2): 475–482.

Forstater, M. 2004. "Green Jobs: Addressing the Critical Issues Surrounding the Environment, Workplace and Employment." *International Journal of Environment, Workplace and Employment,* 1 (1): 53–61.

Garzon de la Roza, G. 2006. "Continued Struggle for Survival: How Plan *Jefes y Jefas* Affected Poor Women's Lives in Greater Buenos Aires, 2002–2005." *Georgetown University Development Management and Policy Program Collection.* http://hdl.handle.net/1961/4188, accessed February 15, 2012.

Harvey, P. 2000. "Direct Job Creation." In Aaron Warner et al. (ed.), *Commitment to Full Employment: Macroeconomics and Social Policy in Memory of William Vickrey,* M.E. Sharpe, 35–54.

IADB. 2005. "Support for the *Plan Familias* Program, Argentina." Inter-American Development Bank Loan Proposal AR-L1006.

Kaboub, F. 2007. "Employment Guarantee Programs: A Survey of Theories and Policy Experiences." *Working Paper 498,* Annandale-on-Hudson, NY: The Levy Economics Institute (May).

Keynes, J. M. 1964[1936]. *The General Theory of Employment, Interest, and Money,* New York: Harcourt-Brace & World, Inc.

Keynes, J. M. 1980. *Activities 1940–46. Shaping the Post-War World: Employment and Commodities.* Volume XXVII of *Collected Works,* D. Moggridge (ed.). London, UK: Palgrave Macmillan.

Keynes, J. M. 1981. *Activities 1922–29. The Return to Gold and Industrial Policy: Part II.* Volume XIX of *Collected Works,* D. Moggridge (ed.). London, UK: Palgrave Macmillan.

Kostzer, D. 2008. "Argentina: A Case Study on the *Plan Jefes y Jefas de Hogar Desocupados,* or the Employment Road to Economic Recovery." Working Paper No. 534. Annandale-on-Hudson, NY: Levy Economics Institute.

Minsky, H. P. 1986. *Stabilizing an Unstable Economy,* New Haven, CT: Yale University Press.

Mitchell, W. F. 1998. "The Buffer Stock Employment Model and the NAIRU: The Path to Full Employment." *Journal of Economic Issues,* 32 (June): 547–556.

Mitchell, W. F. and Wray, L. R. (2005), "In Defense of Employer of Last Resort: a Response to Malcolm Sawyer," *Journal of Economic Issues,* 39(1): 235–245.

Mosler, W. B. 1997–1998. "Full Employment and Price Stability." *Journal of Post Keynesian Economics,* 20 (2): 167–182.

MTEySS. 2002. *Impacto Macroeconómico Del Programa Jefas y Jefes De Hogar,* Buenos Aires, Argentina: Ministerio de Trabajo, Empleo y Seguridad Social, Agosto.

MTEySS. 2003. *Plan Jefas y Jefes de Hogar Desocupados: Un año de gestión, Mayo 2002—Mayo 2003,* Buenos Aires, Argentina: Ministerio de Trabajo, Empleo y Seguridad Social.

MTEySS. 2005. "Segunda Evaluación del Programa Jefes de Hogar. Resultados de la Encuesta a beneficiarios." Buenos Aires, Argentina: Ministerio de Trabajo, Empleo y Seguridad Social.

Pastoret, C. and M. Tepepa. 2006. "Community Development and ELR: A Gender-Aware Perspective and the Jefes and Jefas Program in Argentina." In D. Papadimitriou (ed.) *Employment Guarantee Policies: Theory and Practice.* The Levy Economics Institute Conference Proceedings, presented during October 13–14, 2006 conference on the Employer of Last Resort.

Tcherneva, P. R. 2005. "The Art of Job Creation: Promises and Problems of the Argentinean Experience." C-FEPS Special Report 05/03, Kansas City, MO: Center for Full Employment and Price Stability of the University of Missouri-Kansas City.

Tcherneva, P. R. 2006. "Universal Assurances in the Public Interest: Evaluating the Economic Viability of Basic Income and Job Guarantees." *International Journal of Environment, Workplace, and Employment,* Vol. 2, No. 1, pp. 69–88.

Tcherneva, P. R. 2011. "The Case for Labor Demand Targeting." *Journal of Economic Issues,* June 2011, 45 (2): 401–409.

Tcherneva, P. R. 2012a. "Employer of Last Resort." In J. King (ed.), *Elgar Companion to Post Keynesian Economics,* Northampton, MA: Edward Elgar 161–166.

Tcherneva, P. R. 2012b. "On-the-spot Employment: Keynes's Approach to Full Employment and Economic Transformation," *Review of Social Economy,* 2012, 70 (1): 57–80.

Tcherneva, P. R. and L. R. Wray. 2005a. "Common Goals—Different Solutions: Can Basic Income and Job Guarantees Deliver Their Own Promises?" *Rutgers Journal of Law and Urban Policy,* 2 (1): 125–166.

Tcherneva, P. R. and L. R. Wray. 2005b. "Employer of Last Resort: A Case Study of Argentina's *Jefes* Program." *C-FEPS Working Paper No. 41,* Kansas City, MO: Center for Full Employment and Price Stability of the University of Missouri-Kansas City.

Tcherneva, P. R. and L. R. Wray. 2005c. "Is Argentina's *Jefes de Hogar* an Employer of Last Resort Program?" *C-FEPS Working Paper No. 43,* Kansas City, MO: Center for Full Employment and Price Stability of the University of Missouri-Kansas City.

Tcherneva, P. R. and L. R. Wray. 2005d. "Gender and the Job Guarantee: The Impact of Argentina's *Jefes* Program on Female Heads of Households." *C-FEPS Working Paper No. 49,* Kansas City, MO: Center for Full Employment and Price Stability of the University of Missouri-Kansas City.

World Bank. 2002. "Project Appraisal Document on a Proposed Loan in the Amount of US$600 Million to the Argentine Republic for the Jefes De Hogar (Heads of Household) Program Project." *World Bank Report No. 23710-AR.* October 22.

World Bank. 2003. "Implementation Completion Report (SCL-43660) on a Loan in the Amount of US$284 Million Equivalent to the Argentine Republic for a Third Social Protection Project." *World Bank Report No. 26134-AR.* June 30.

Wray, L. R. 1998. Understanding Modern Money: The Key to Full Employment and Price Stability. Cheltenham, UK: Edward Elgar.

CHAPTER 4

Employment Generation Schemes and Long-Term Development: A Case Study of the NREGA in India

Poulomi Dasgupta

One of the key objectives of governments of developing countries is to ensure that their most disadvantaged people come out of poverty and live better lives. The role of a government in this case should be not only to help people get access to resources that are required to gain material well-being, but also to offer people job opportunities when the market is unable to offer fruitful employment.

The National Rural Employment Guarantee Act (NREGA) is an employment-generation program enacted by legislation in India in 2005 in order to guarantee employment to the poorest section of the society. The chapter investigates the impact of the NREGA on economic development in India. In order to carry out this analysis, village-level surveys were conducted. A qualitative approach has been taken to evaluate the impact of the act on economic development using Sen's (1997, 2004) capabilities approach.

The organization of the chapter is as follows: the second section introduces the readers to the NREGA and its salient features; the third section gives a detailed description of the village-level surveys and their basic findings; the fourth section examines the capability approach to development; the fifth section employs the capability approach in evaluating the impact of NREGA on development; and the sixth section concludes the chapter by advancing the argument that the impact of NREGA should be examined based on a broader understanding of development.

The National Rural Employment Guarantee Act

NREGA was initiated in 2006 in 200 Indian districts to address the growing concerns regarding increasing unemployment and underemployment in the rural sectors of the country and has since been expanded to cover 630 districts. Unemployment and "out of the labor force" days for rural agricultural workers is 104 days per year. The number of agricultural workers went up from 7.08 million in 1981 to 121 million in 2008 (Sharma, 2010). There exists chronic poverty in many districts of the country.

The aim of NREGA is to enhance the livelihood of rural workers by guaranteeing up to 100 days of wage employment within 15 days of application. The program intends to provide jobs in order to create durable assets for the rural poor, in areas such as water conservation, irrigation canals, drought proofing, and so on. The number of households given employment was 21 million in 2006 and increased to over 52 million in 2010.

Jean Drèze (2008) suggests that this act would give opportunities to enhance the livelihoods of the rural population: "In particular this Act can help to break the 'dictatorship of the private employer'." Rural workers are forced to accept exploitative wages and working conditions. The implementation of the act offers the rural poor the ability to organize themselves in order to get better wages from private employers and enhance their well-being.

The introduction of NREGA has brought a new dimension to development programs in India. Since it ensures the right to employment, the hierarchy between the government as the provider and the participants as recipients has been greatly challenged. The government also falls under the law and is now accountable for inefficiencies in the implementation of the program.

NREGA also provides for a 33 percent participation rate of women in its projects. The participation rate of women has surpassed the provision in the act. In 2010–2011, for example, women participated in NREGA projects at the rate of 48 percent at the all India level. The greater inclusion of women under this act has an impact at two levels: additional income to the household and greater decision-making power at the household level. Sharma (2010) explains, "This self-targeting, with no criteria of poverty and employment, and with the flexibility to drop in and drop out makes it easy for women to participate." Various studies

(Dasgupta and Sudarshan 2011) have shown that women have a greater incentive to participate in this program because of predictable working hours, better working conditions, and so on.

NREGA does not discriminate between people based on their caste and social backgrounds.[1] The participation of the people from Scheduled Castes (SCs), Scheduled Tribes (STs), and below poverty line (BPL) families has been encouraging. Indeed, SCs accounted for 30 percent and STs for 21 percent of person-days created in 2009–2010. In communities where discrimination limits employment opportunities in the private sector, villages with higher percentages of SC and ST communities have organized themselves into local self-help groups to take advantage of the provisions under NREGA.

NREGA is implemented by agencies at six different levels of the government. These levels, from the lowest to the highest, are the village, the village cluster, the block, the district, the state, and the central government. Each agency is given a set of rights and obligations to ensure the effective implementation of the act. The agency at the village level, referred to as the Gram Sabha, has the right to determine the various projects they will undertake and to conduct social audits. The Gram Sabha is also obligated to formulate projects and demand work based on the needs of its participants. Gram Panchayat (GP), the agency at the village-cluster level, is responsible for consolidating recommendations from the various Gram Sabhas and is required, among other things, to issue job cards and allocate work. At the block level, the office of the program officer has the right to consolidate GP plans into block plans and to receive funds for these projects. This office is also required to address grievances within seven days of any complaint. At the district level, the District Program Coordinator consolidates block plans and receives funds for them. They are also expected to ensure proactive disclosure. At the state level, the Department of Rural Development has the right to formulate schemes, receive funds from the central government, monitor, and evaluate. The state government is required to fund 25 percent of the material costs and to pay unemployment allowance. At the highest level, the Ministry of Rural Development has the right to make amendments to the law while the central council has the right to monitor, evaluate, and collect statistics. The central government is required to fund 100 percent of the costs incurred for wages and 75 percent of the material costs and release central funds on time to the various agencies that implement the program (Sharma, 2010).

The agencies at each level of government have a set of certain rights and obligations under the act. The ability to enforce their rights gives them access to the various resources necessary to implement the act. The obligations of the various agencies allows for a transparent and effective implementation of the act.

Essential to the efficiency of the act are its provisions to ensure transparency. These include proactive disclosure (including the availability of records at the GP and in the public domain), social audits by Gram Sabhas, the redressing of grievances, and the issuing of penalties. Monitoring the act involves cross verification of government records with realities on the ground. NREGA requires regular audits be made in the Gram Sabhas at least once every six months that consist of interviews with the card holders and verifying the information that is on their job cards and gathering information about the projects that have been started under NREGA. The auditors share their findings with the job seekers at public meetings in the audited village and the information (e.g., the amount of wages disbursed) that is available through government records is verified with the information gathered from the participants of the act. This process helps limit local corruption in the disbursement of funds. A study of social audits in the state of Andhra Pradesh by Aiyar and Samji (2009) revealed that social audits led to a dramatic increase in the awareness of the provisions in the act. This decentralization ensures greater accountability from the various government agencies involved.

NREGA has been instrumental in redefining the process of development in India. While earlier development programs were based mainly on the objective of increasing welfare via handout schemes and cash transfers, NREGA combines two important aspects of development: access to income via creation of jobs, thereby using the underutilized labor resources of the country, and the creation of physical infrastructure and physical assets in the rural areas. Most development programs are aimed at poverty alleviation of the poorest sections of society. Because NREGA is a rights-based act, it makes development a two-step process: it first makes the government liable for the implementation of the act and then helps communities and local governing bodies become crucial in the development process.

Field Surveys and Findings

For a more comprehensive look at the program, four short-term field surveys of NREGA were conducted in order to gauge the impact of the act on its participants. The states of Haryana and West Bengal were selected on the basis of the number of person-days they had generated under the program. One of the main reasons for selecting these two states was the fact that Haryana's performance in implementing this program has been relatively better than West Bengal's in many areas.[2] West Bengal has been one of the worst-performing states in the country so far.

Village-level surveys were conducted in these two states. The surveys consisted of personal interviews with the beneficiaries of NREGA as well as with the village heads.[3] The interview questions were open-ended to allow for detailed responses from those interviewed. Every attempt was made to control for gender bias by including both men and women as participants in the survey.

The surveys were conducted at two different levels. An exploratory survey was conducted at a single village in Haryana and a more detailed survey was conducted in West Bengal with surveys being conducted in three different villages. The surveys were short term in nature.[4] The interviews focused both on economic indicators that included the impact of the additional income earned on the consumption expenditure and on noneconomic indicators. These included the impact of the program on the daily lives of the participants as a direct result of the physical assets created under the program and the level of community involvement in determining the kind of work to be done. The act aims to increase the number of person-days per household. Table 4.1 illustrates the average number of person-days created in the two states since the implementation of the act.

In terms of the average number of person-days per household, Haryana's performance was significantly higher than West Bengal's each year since the start of the program except in 2009–2010 and 2010–2011. Though neither state had been able to create anywhere close to 100 days of employment, Haryana's performance was closer to the best-performing states.

The act aims to target the poorest sections of the rural populations. Additionally, it aims to reach the most disadvantaged people, which

Table 4.1 Average person-days per household

	2006–2007	*2007–2008*	*2008–2009*	*2009–2010*	*2010–2011*	*2011–2012*
Haryana	48	49	42.41	37.74	35.79	30.85
West Bengal	14	18	26	33.42	31.07	14.45

Source: www.nrega.nic.in.

Table 4.2 Participation of marginalized groups

	Percent of SC participation	*Percent of ST participation*	*Percent of women participation*
Haryana	53.61	0	34.81
West Bengal	36.86	14.38	33.42

Source: www.nrega.nic.in.

include women and SC members. The participation of disadvantaged groups in these two states for the year 2009–2010 can be seen in the table 4.2.

Participation of disadvantaged groups in NREGA has been comparable in both states. While the participation of SCs was higher in Haryana than in West Bengal, it should be noted that the participation of ST groups in Haryana is zero because its ST population is negligible. The participation of women was comparable in both the states.

One of the more difficult issues within the scope of the act is the determination of wages. The economic rationale behind employment generation programs is to offer wages below the existing market rate or minimum wage rates so that labor resources are not drawn away from the private sector. Real wages under NREGA are delinked from minimum wage rates and are rather adjusted for inflation using the consumer price index (Agricultural Laborers) (table 4.3).

Village 1: Haryana[5]

This village, located in district of Mewat in Nuh block, is a part of Salamba Village Panchayat or Gram Panchayat and is in close proximity (about 45 kilometers) to Gurgoan, a highly urbanized area close to the national capital of New Delhi, to which it is connected by state highway 13. There are regular bus services between Gurgoan and Nuh.

Table 4.3 Wage rate under NREGA

	2007–2008	*2008–2009*	*2009–2010*	*Revised wages*	*Minimum wages for agricultural workers*
Haryana	135	141.02	141.02	179	167
West Bengal	69.43	75	100	130	96

Source: Sharma, 2010.

Nevertheless, in order to get to the village one has to walk or use a private vehicle from the highway. Most villagers walk, as they do not have access to private vehicles.

Eighty-five percent of the population in this village are Mayos and the remaining are non-Mayos. The average family size is 9.5. One of the main problems faced by this village is an acute shortage of water. Water tables are unusable for human consumption because water is not potable. Drinking water is bought by villagers from private water tankers that come to the villages on a weekly basis. Expenditure on water is significant.

The village has 264 households that have registered for jobs under the program. Of these, eight are BPL. The total number of people registered under the program is 483, and 20 people were interviewed during the survey of this village. Of these, 15 were men and 5 women. All the male respondents were involved in two main economic activities: during agricultural cycles they worked as daily agricultural workers and during the off-season they migrated to nearby towns to work as construction workers, rickshaw pullers, and so on. When in such towns, they typically did not have any accommodations and would generally sleep on footpaths or other open spaces. Of the people interviewed none was a landowner, but they sometimes worked on land leased to them by landowners to grow mustard, wheat, and fodder for animals. Women typically stay at home to attend to household chores but are also involved in collecting fodder for animals and collecting drinking water for cooking and other household chores.

Impact of NREGA

Of the 20 people interviewed, all were able to secure 52 days of work under the program in 2010–2011, which was higher than the state average of 35.7 days for the same year. Payments to the workers were made on time. Of the 15 men interviewed, all found the income earned under the act was insufficient to support their families during the lean seasons; 12 of them agreed that if 100 days of work were provided as the act directs, their financial state would be much less precarious. The remaining three added that better organization was needed to demand for work and improve the situation of the workers. There had been no significant change in migration since the implementation of the act. With the exception of the women interviewed, all the men said that they still had to go to nearby big cities to look for work. Only a few of the respondents indicated that their household debts had decreased slightly since they started working under the act.

The projects that were undertaken were the creation of unpaved roads and the creation of rainwater catchment areas for water conservation; 250 people were able to procure work in the NREGA projects in 2010–2011. In this particular village, unpaved roads were recently constructed. Since the survey was conducted during the summer months, one could not establish the impact monsoons would have on the unpaved roads. The catchment areas were considered as the most valuable assets created under the act. The female respondents found the creation of these assets especially valuable.

This survey was aimed to investigate the impact of NREGA on the participants at two levels. The 20 people who were interviewed during this phase of the survey revealed that the impact of the wages paid under the act was insufficient to significantly change their consumption patterns. However, the impact of the asset creation on the quality of life seemed to be much more significant. This was especially the case for creation of catchment areas for rainwater. Based on these findings, more detailed surveys of three villages were conducted in West Bengal. Since the survey in Haryana did not indicate a significant impact on incomes or consumption expenditure, the second round of surveys concentrated more on the assets created under the act and the economic and noneconomic impacts of these assets on the participants.

Village 2: West Bengal

This village is situated in the Bolpur-Sriniketan block of Birbhum district and is part of Kasba Gram Panchayat, which consists of 10 villages. About 4,642 households were registered under the act; of these 22 were BPL. The village consisted of 186 households and 900 people; 25 people were interviewed in this village. Of these 25, 7 were women and 18 men. All the respondents had participated in NREGA in the previous year. All the male respondents were farmers, but none were landowners, so all of them leased land from bigger landowners during harvest season. The landowners provided the farmers with seeds and fertilizers while the cost of all other inputs were borne by the farmers. The two main crop cycles in this region are rice and mustard. Most of the farmers in this village were subsistence farmers. Occasionally, they were able to sell their produce at local markets and their grains to the local grain mills. During lean seasons, most of the male respondents typically found work in neighboring towns as construction workers and masons. All the women respondents were involved in household work and did not seek work out side of the villages.

Impact of NREGA

Of the 25 people interviewed, all were able to find around 25–30 days of work, which was slightly lower than the state average of 31.07 days for the same year. Payments were made on time. Of the 18 men interviewed, 14 indicated that the additional income provided by the act (while making only a marginal difference in their consumption patterns) helped them meet their basic household needs and made it unnecessary for them to seek jobs in urban areas during the lean seasons. Some of the respondents also said that while there was a demand for jobs, there was not enough work for the creation of assets generated under the act.

The projects undertaken in this village consisted mainly of the building of roads and the creation of catchment areas for rainwater. Four unpaved roads were built to connect the village to the neighboring villages and to the main highway. A concrete road, 600 meters long, was also built to connect two schools. Three catchment areas were constructed under this act, each of which had rainwater in them during the survey period. Of these three, two were for irrigation of agricultural land and one was for providing water for household purposes like washing clothes and dishes while also being used to breed fish for the consumption of village residents. Despite the improvement in the availability of water, agriculture is still heavily dependent on monsoons. The survey was undertaken after a good year of rainfall, which had a significant impact on the usefulness of the assets created under the act.

Of the seven women interviewed, one was actively involved in the village-level planning of asset creation in the village. Each said that they had been able to earn some additional income for their families under the act.

Village 3: West Bengal

This village is also located in the Bolpur-Sriniketan block and is part of the Bahiri Panchshowa Gram Panchayat; 454 households in this village were registered under the act and 24 people were interviewed in this village.[6] Of them, 14 were women and 10 men. The main economic activity of this village was agriculture and all the respondents were landless agricultural workers. Some of the respondents were involved in petty trade like basket weaving. Some of the women respondents also worked in nearby towns as maids.

Impact of NREGA

All 24 respondents had worked under the act in the previous year. None of the respondents indicated a significant difference in income and consumption due to the income earned through the act. Payments were made on time.

Pond excavation was the primary asset-creation project undertaken in the previous year with the NREGA funds. Once the catchment area was created, the local GP and self-help groups initiated a two-stage program of land leveling and social forestry. From a total of 25,000[7] rupees, 20 percent of these funds were invested by the local self-help groups[8] and the remaining 80 percent by the GP. Under this two-stage process, kitchen gardens were planted around the pond created under NREGA. Various vegetables like lady's fingers and bitter gourds and fruits like bananas, papayas, and lemons were grown around the pond. The pond itself was the main source of irrigation. Manure for the kitchen garden was supplied by the local vermin compost. Fish harvesting was also undertaken with the help of the local self-help groups. All the vegetables and fish were sold in the local markets. Earnings from these sales were additional income for the households who are directly involved in the maintenance of the kitchen garden and vermicompost bin. The participants of the survey also said that the next step in the project was to invest in chickens and ducks in order to sell their eggs in the local markets.

All the respondents were involved in the creation of the pond under NREGA. The income earned via the program had made marginal changes in their overall income. However, the asset created under the scheme was found to be much more valuable due to the economic opportunities that were generated. All the respondents also agreed on the importance of community work and cooperation between the GP and the local self-groups in the development of this project. Of all the villages surveyed, this was the only one in which more women participated in the program than men. Employment was also given to two people who were handicapped.

Village 4: West Bengal

This village is located in the Bolpur-Sriniketan block and is part of the Kankalitala Gram Panchayat, which consists of 15 villages. A total of 4,248 households were registered under the act in this GP. This village has 282 households and a total population of 1,333 people; 15 people were interviewed in this village, 12 of whom were men and three women. All the respondents had participated in NREGA during the previous year. All the men were daily agricultural workers. Unlike the other villages surveyed, this village had only one harvest season the previous year. During off-seasons, most of the respondents had to seek work at local brick kilns. One of the main concerns of the people in this village was an acute shortage of drinking water.

Impact of NREGA

Respondents indicated that they were able to secure only about 10–15 days of work in the previous year. One of the main complaints of the respondents was with the delay in payments, which they said were delayed sometimes up to six months. They were paid a daily wage of 130 rupees per day, however, because the person-days created under the act were so few in this village, the income earned under this program was not significant. Another concern voiced by the participants of this survey was that the contractors in charge of procuring material for the projects under the act would often bring their own workers.

Asset creation was very poor in this village. They had created two catchment areas for rainwater in the previous year, but because the work on them had started after the monsoons, neither had much water in them. In addition, most respondents said that there was a lack of interest at the GP level to create more assets and implement the program more efficiently due to the political affiliation of the village.

Capability Approach to Development

One of the pertinent issues for such an ambitious program is the impact it has on its participants. Access to employment is crucial for the economic and social well-being of individuals. How does an act that guarantees rights-based employment contribute to the process of development itself? In order to answer this question, we must first understand what development means given our particular context.

Fukuda-Parr (2003) writes about three different approaches to development: the neoliberal alternative, the basic needs antecedent, and the human development approach. The concept of well-being according to the neoliberal alternative, says Fukuda-Parr, is that of utility maximization and is primarily concerned with economic growth and efficiency. The measurement tools for this approach are aggregate measures like

GDP growth and per capita income. The key operational goal for this approach is economic growth. Under this approach the individual is the fundamental agent and human resources are means for economic activity.

Basic needs antecedent is fundamentally different from the previous approach. According to Fukuda-Parr, the concept of well-being under this approach entails meeting basic needs. The main evaluative tool is poverty reduction by means of income and access to basic social tools. This approach is concerned with expanding social services via stronger political will.

However, it is the third approach—the human development approach—which has radicalized the way development has been perceived since the end of World War II. This approach has criticized the narrow understanding of development and the emphasis on growth rates of GDP for development and well-being. We adopt this approach, which is founded upon the capability approach. This approach encourages us to think of development from a different and a more useful perspective.

Developed by Amartya Sen, the capability approach provides a foundation to understand the process of development. Sen's contribution came as a critique to the utilitarian framework for evaluating welfare and development.

> Development can be seen, it is argued here, as a process of expanding the real freedoms that people enjoy. Focusing on human freedoms contrasts with narrower views of development, such as identifying development with the growth of gross national product, or with the rise of personal incomes or with industrialization, or with technological advance or with social modernization.
>
> (Sen, 1999, p. 3)

The main focus of Sen's approach is to expand the notion of development from a narrow focus on utility maximization and meeting basic needs for human survival. According to this approach, development should be understood in terms of people's capability to function, to have access to opportunities to undertake activities, which they themselves value for their own well-being. This approach is a normative approach. According to Sen, there are two main aspects to the capability approach: functioning and capability. Sen (1997) explains functionings as follows: "The concept of functionings . . . reflects the various things a person may value doing or being." Valued functioning according to Sen will vary from individual to individual; it can range from being adequately nourished to being able to take part in community life. Valued functioning is the direct result of one's physical and social environment.

Capability on the other hand refers to the "alternative combinations" of functionings that are feasible for an individual to achieve. Sen gives the example of an affluent person who fasts and of a destitute person who is forced to starve. In both the cases, the achieved functioning is the same: neither eats. In the case of the affluent person, however, fasting was a matter of choice. He or she was free to choose from a variety of alternative functionings, whereas the destitute person had no choice in the achieved functioning.

Sen (1997) explains, "The set of alternative functioning vectors available to her for choice is called her capability set. While the combinations of functionings . . . a person undertakes reflects her achievements, the capability set represents the freedom to achieve: the alternative functioning combinations from which this person can choose" (p. 75).

According to the capability approach then, development should be an expansion of these freedoms, an expansion of the capability set an individual faces. Using this approach, Sen points out that if development is indeed expansion of an individual's freedom, then one has to distinguish between human beings as means and ends for development.

> Seeing human qualities in terms of their importance in promoting and sustaining economic growth, significant as it is, tells us nothing about why economic growth is sought after in the first place, nor much about the role of enhanced human qualities in making it directly possible for us to lead a freer and more fulfilling lives.

Sen argues that instead of looking at human beings as a means to end, we must focus on the direct impact of social policies on their lives. For example, the expansion of social services like healthcare and education should be considered as "developmental" since they allow individuals to have more "freedoms." Increase in labor productivity and actual production commodities as a result of such social policies should be purely a secondary focus. "Indeed," he explains, "even as far as expansion of commodity production is concerned, it has to be borne in mind that they are valued, ultimately, not for their own sake, but as means to human welfare and freedom" (Sen, 1997).

The building blocks of the capability approach are as follows: commodities, conversion factors, capability set, agency/choice, and functioning or achieved functioning (Robeyns, 2005). There are goods and services that by themselves may not offer much to an individual. These goods and services have to be converted into something that might be of more use to the individual involved. These goods and services can be called as either capability inputs or commodities. Various conversion factors are required to convert these capability inputs into "functionings," defined as "beings and doings that are valued by individuals." Robeyns explains there are three groups of conversion factors: personal conversion factors, which include one's metabolism, physical condition, reading skills, intelligence, and others; social conversion factors, which include public policies and social norms; and environmental conversion factors, which include climate, geographical location, among others.

The next building block is that of a capability set. The capability set refers to an alternative combination of functionings. The capability set for an individual will consist of many different combinations of functionings. Sen restrains from giving a list of capabilities that individuals value. According to him, capability set consists of many different possible functionings and this set is determined based on what the individual finds valuable for their own well-being. Sen does mention "basic capabilities," which are a subset of all capabilities. In Sen's work, basic capabilities refer to the freedom of access to some basic things that are necessary for survival and to escape poverty. Robeyns (2005) explains,

> While the notion of capabilities refers to a very broad range, basic capabilities refer to the real opportunity to avoid poverty. Basic capabilities will thus be crucial for poverty analysis and more generally for studying the well-being of the majority of people in developing countries (p.101).

One of the key benefits of the capability approach is that it can be used to evaluate freedoms and development in affluent societies as well. It is in this case that the set of functionings that form the capability set tends to become much more complex and normative in nature.

An analysis of conversion factors usually refers to external impediments to the ability of individuals to convert basic inputs into capabilities. While the actual selection of a particular functioning from the capability set is often seen as an individual matter, the choice may be influenced by a set of social and cultural norms. Robeyns (2005) argues, "It is, however, important to question to what extent people have genuinely access to all the capabilities in their capability set."

Having discussed the building blocks of the capability approach, we will now use this approach to evaluate the impact of NREGA on the development and well-being of individuals who have participated in the scheme.

Using Capability Approach to Evaluate NREGA

The first step is to identify the capability input in rural sectors in India that can be converted into a possible capability set. We assume the existence of underutilized labor resources as the capability input for the reason that majority of rural workers do not own land or own very little land and therefore do not have access to any sources of livelihood other than their own labor power. For example, the percentage of land holdings under small or marginal farmers went up from 70 percent in 1970 to 82 percent in 2001 (Sharma, 2010). In the surveys conducted by this author, more than 90 percent of the respondents did not own land and were mainly daily wage workers. In such a case, rural workers' main source of livelihood is their labor power. According to Sen (1981), "Work and income we receive in return for selling our labour power generates functionings, capabilities and ultimately utility for employed person." Precarious employment opportunities not only affect the income of most rural workers, but also contracts their capability set. For the purposes of our analysis, unused and underutilized labor sources are therefore the primary capability input.

The next building block in our analysis is the conversion factor. In our case, the conversion factor is a social conversion factor in the form of a public policy, that is, the NREGA. This act ensures a right to employment and can therefore be seen as a conversion factor because it gives the unused and underutilized labor power of rural workers access to fruitful employment opportunities. Job creation also results in an expansion of the capability set of individuals. Both job creation and the utilization of unused physical resources like land and water to create assets for the rural poor have led to an expansion of the capability set of the rural population.

A point of contention is a value judgment associated with the determination of a capability set. Sen, for instance, argues that in order to assess social policy, we must pay attention to individual formulations of well-being. Sen has consistently refrained from providing a list of functionings that should be considered a universal list of capabilities. As a result, some of the most common questions that come up while using the capability approach are which capabilities matter and how are they determined. Martha Nussbaum, who has criticized Sen for not endorsing a universal list of capabilities, has offered a universal set of her own consisting of ten categories: life; bodily health; bodily integrity; senses, imagination, and thought; emotions; practical reason; affiliation; other species; play; and control over one's environment (as cited in Robeyns, 2005). However,

Sen's response (2004) to such criticism is that it is not the job of a theorist to cement a universal list of capabilities. According to him, "(P)ure theory cannot 'freeze' a list of capabilities for all societies for all time to come, irrespective of what the citizen comes to understand and value. That would be not only a denial of the reach of democracy, but also a misunderstanding of what pure theory can do, completely divorced from the particular social reality that any particular society faces" (Sen, 2004). Therefore Sen focuses more on public discussion and democratic debate in determining a list of capabilities within a given societal framework.

Unterhalter (2003) explains, "Governments using the capability approach therefore have an obligation to establish and sustain conditions for each and every individual, irrespective of gender, ethnicity, race or regional location, to achieve valued outcomes. These may entail acquiring a certain level of educational attainment, but they undoubtedly entail ensuring the freedoms that allow valued outcomes to be articulated and achieved."

Within the context of NREGA, the key is to understand that capability set consists of outcomes that are valued by participants of the program. In using this approach we have taken the opportunity to interact with the participants of the program to learn what they value for their well-being.

As part of the surveys, participants were asked how NREGA had impacted their lives and well-being, through the creation of jobs and assets for the rural economy. Their responses have been used in making a list of capabilities for the participants of this program. It should be noted, however, that this list is not an exhaustive list, but only a subset of all the possible functionings that individuals value.

For example, when participants were asked whether the additional income from the program had enabled them to change their expenditure pattern and whether that was important for them, they all responded that the program had improved their ability to earn additional income and to secure jobs close to their homes. All the respondents also said that they valued the fact that they were now able to demand work from the government when they were unemployed. The capability set for women also showed some degree of expansion. For example, when women were asked what positive changes they observed in their lives that they valued since the introduction of the program, they named their ability to participate in decision making at home, to earn additional income for the family, and to take better care of their children. In other words, the impact of job creation under this act gave them a sense of freedom to choose between earning additional income when needed or staying at home when required. Most of the women who were interviewed during the survey said that they could not seek work out of their villages due to social and infrastructural restrictions. Because jobs generated by NREGA gave them the freedom to work in their own villages if they wished, if a woman remains at home to take care of her children, she does so out of choice rather than compulsion.

Asset creation also affected the expansion of their capabilities.[9] For example, when asked about the usefulness of unpaved roads in the villages, many villagers responded that they could now get to a hospital in case of an emergency more quickly than before. Easy access to healthcare was particularly highly valued in village 2. Additionally, some respondents in village 2 explained that unpaved roads provided better access to local markets to sell their products. This was previously not possible due to inferior rural connectivity. Better access to schools was yet another valued functioning of the program's infrastructure development. Another addition to the capability set was the ability of the participants to create more sources of incomes, through the creation of assets under the act. Village 3, for example, valued this ability to create additional avenues of income. Respondents from village 2, for example, valued the ability to irrigate their farms with the help of rainwater catchment areas created under the act.

Asset creation also had a significant impact on women. When asked whether their lives had improved because of the creation of these assets, the majority responded positively to the creation of catchment areas. Most women highly valued their ability to access water easily for their household chores. This was particularly important for the women, because many of them had to spend a considerable amount of time getting water for household chores in the days prior to the creation of the assets. Their ability to have easy access to water was a valued functioning for them as it enabled them to spend more time with their children and take better care of them.

About 90 percent of the participants indicated that their capability set had indeed expanded since the implementation of the act. In terms of the capability approach, participants of the program were given more functionings to choose from to better their lives.

One of the main problems that researchers face when using the capability approach is whether to evaluate expansion of the capability set or the actual functionings achieved. For example, Unterhalter (2003) states,

> Sometimes it is important to assess functionings rather than capabilities, for example in a situation where schooling has been withdrawn from

> certain groups, as happened in Afghanistan under the Taliban or in South Africa under apartheid. But assessing functionings, rather than capabilities, can be very misleading, especially when making comparisons between people in different social circumstances. A malnourished woman in Malawi has a different capability set than a self-starved British model (p.6).

In our case, however, we must distinguish between the achieved functioning due to direct creation of jobs and the creation of assets. The reason for this distinction is as follows.

We have already established that there had been an expansion of the capability set of participants as a result of the creation of jobs and assets under the act. Achieved functionings, however, are relatively more difficult to observe in case of the impact of direct job creation. When respondents were asked after the implementation of the act, of all the functionings that they now had access to, which ones they actually chose, the answers were varied. For example, most respondents chose to demand for work by applying for job cards and registering themselves under the program. When asked why they did not assert their right to the 100 days of work guaranteed by the act, despite their expressed desire for it, they cited lack of projects or poor planning by local governing bodies. The implication is that while NREGA has expanded the capability set of the participants, social and political factors have disallowed them from selecting freely from it. In the case of village 4, for example, participants were unable to assert their choice to work and earn income under the act because of their political affiliation.

Though the responses in the case of achieved functionings were varied, some commonalities that were observed were participants demanding work, participants choosing to work on projects generated under the act rather than migrate to close by towns, and women making use of the act to earn additional income.

The functionings achieved through asset creation was more evident in some villages than others. For example, in village 3, the ability to create additional sources of income from the assets created under the act was actually achieved. As mentioned earlier, because of the involvement of local self-help groups, kitchen gardens were planted around the pond that was created under the act. These then generated both additional sources of income and basic consumption goods for their own consumption. Individuals chose to make a common decision with regard to creation of additional sources of income with the help of the assets created under the act.

In village 2, participants had started to make irrigation canals from the rainwater catchment areas to irrigate their lands. Realizing their capability to irrigate their farms gave them greater control over their harvests. In the cases of both villages 2 and 3, social influence on individual decision-making processes allowed participants to realize the functionings they valued as a community.[10]

From the primary data collected from these four villages, we can conclude that while there has been a definite expansion in the capability set of the participants in these villages, their achieved functioning varies from village to village and was due to differences in the implementation of the program, the inefficiency in resource allocation, and political differences.

Conclusion

Based on our findings above, we contend that the impact of an employment guarantee act like NREGA should be evaluated on terms broader than traditional evaluative indicators like income and consumption expenditure. It is not that these indicators are unimportant, but income and growth rates show only a partial picture of the actual impact of a program like the NREGA.

Why is it important for us to broaden our understanding of development when evaluating social policies like employment generation programs? Like other developing countries, India has embarked upon a neoliberal path to achieve high growth rates. As a result, there has been a move toward fiscal austerity and cuts in spending for welfare programs. In such an economic climate, it is easy to lose sight of the impact of an ambitious program like the NREGA. A number of critics have claimed that a program like NREGA is only a drain on government funds and tax payer money. Indicators like number of person-days created under the program are often cited as evidence against the program. Though it is true that the average of 30–35 person-days is far below the 100 days guaranteed by the act, nevertheless, there was a significant expansion in the capability set of the individuals interviewed. The expansion of one's capability set or freedom to choose from various functionings is important for the well-being of individuals. When the capability approach is employed, individuals become the center of analysis.

Sen (1999) describes this approach as,

> This freedom centered understanding of economics and of the process of development is very much an agent-oriented view. With adequate social opportunities, individuals can effectively shape their own destiny and help each other. They need not be seen primarily as passive recipients of the benefits of cunning development programs. There is indeed a strong rationale for recognizing the positive role of free and sustainable agency.

Yet another reason for using the capability approach to evaluate a program like NREGA is in the design of the act itself. As discussed earlier, the act provides for its implementation and monitoring in a variety of ways. For example, there is a great degree of decentralization in the planning process. Determining what projects need to be undertaken at the village level and how they should be implemented requires participation at both the agency and individual levels, thus making the act more democratic and less prone to corruption. Decentralization has made the implementation of the act a responsibility of the participants as well. The participants have been given the right to not only demand for work, but they also get an opportunity to become active members in the process of development of their own communities. Additionally, the act's monitoring system allows for a greater transparency and more efficient allocation. The act gives its participants greater access to income while also enabling them to use their community ties to stimulate the rural economy via different channels. It allows for greater space for debate between participants at the village level and encourages grassroots level democracy.

There is no doubt that there is corruption at some levels of governance and wasted resources. However, the act itself allows for a great expansion of individual's capabilities, which will enhance and improve its implementation.

Employment generation schemes have been part of economic thought for a long time now. Unused labor resources are the key to stimulating the process of development in a country like India. Employment generation not only helps alleviate poverty, but also contributes to the general well-being of a society. Job guarantees give a sense of security to the participants while also expanding their freedom. It allows for the creation of assets crucial to the well-being of the rural poor.

Employment generation programs should be looked upon not only as a way to alleviate poverty, but also as an engine to propel the rural economy of the country in the direction of greater development.

Notes

1. SCs and STs in India are historically disadvantaged groups. Since independence the constitution of India has recognized these groups and has made provisions, including affirmative action, for their development and progress.
2. Rajasthan and Madhya Pradesh have been the best-performing states in terms of average person-days generated.
3. The village head also known as the *Sarpanch* is an elected head of the village or the Gram Sabha.

4. The short-term nature of the surveys is a limitation of the study. A larger number of villages were therefore surveyed to get a more generalized reaction to the program. The focus of the survey was to investigate whether there were any commonalities in the assessments of the program under consideration across the country.
5. While the district, block, and the GPs have been identified in this study, villages have not been identified in accordance with the SSIRB requirements to ensure privacy of the respondents.
6. All the respondents in this survey were part of the ST community. Most villages in this area are divided into *paras* or neighborhoods. Each neighborhood typically constitutes people of one particular caste or tribe.
7. US$1 is about INR50.
8. Self-help groups are groups of 5–20 people of the same low level of economic conditions living in the same locality or hamlet. Participation is voluntary. These groups meet periodically to oversee the weekly or monthly savings of the members and utilize those funds for local development projects.
9. The responses of individuals from each village tended to coincide with their covillagers. This is not surprising, as the various environmental and social factors that are involved in determining one's capabilities will influence individuals who live in a similar surrounding. In our case, it is the village unit.
10. Please refer to Table 16, page 114 in, Dasgupta, P. (2013). *Employment generation program and long term development. The case of India's National Rural Employment Guarantee Act*. Ph.D. Dissertation. http://hdl.handle.net/10355/33222

Bibliography

Aiyar, Y. & Samji, S. (2009). Transparency and Accountability in NREGA: A Case Study of Andhra Pradesh. *Accountability Initiative*, Working Paper No. 1, February 2009.

Alkire, S. (2007). Why the Capability Approach? *Journal of Human Development and Capabilities*, Vol. 6, No. 1, pp. 115–135.

Bhaduri, A. (1999). *On the Border of Economic Theory and History*. New York: Oxford University Press.

Bhaduri, A. (2005). Macroeconomic Policies for Higher Employment in the Era of Globalization. *Employment strategy Papers*, ILO.

Burchardt, F. A. (1944). Foreword. In *The Economics of Full Employment*. Oxford Institute of Economics and Statistics. Oxford: Basil Blackwell.

Chandrasekhar, C. P. (2008). Re-visiting the Policy Environment for Engendering Employment Intensive Economic Growth. Draft paper, *International Labour Office, Geneva.*

Dasgupta, S. & Sudarshan, R. (2011). Issues in Labour Market Inequality and Women's Participation in India's National Rural Employment Guarantee

Programme. *Policy Integration Department, International Labour Office,* International Labour Organization.

Drèze, J. and Sen, A. (1989). *Hunger and Public Action.* Oxford: Oxford University Press. Retrieved from www.capabilityapproach.com/pubs/Maitreyee10_February_08.pdf

Drèze, J. (2008). Employment and Empowerment. In *Maitryee,* Human Development Capability Association.

Forstater, M. (2006). Presentation at Levy Conference on ELR, October.

Fukuda-Parr, S. (2003), The Human Development Paradigm: Operationalizing Sen's Ideas on Capabilities. *Feminist Economics,* Vol. 9, No. 2–3, pp. 301–317.

Ghosh, J. (2002). Macroeconomic Reforms and a Labour Policy Framework for India. *Employment Strategy papers,* International Labor Organization.

Goerne, A. (2010). The Capability Approach in Social Policy Analysis. Yet Another Concept? *Reconciliation of Work and Welfare In Europe Working paper 03.*

Hirway, I. (2006). Enhancing Livelihood Security through the National Employment Guarantee Act: Toward effective implementation of the act. *Levy Economics Institute Working Paper,* No. 434, www.levy.org

Kaboub, F. (2007). Employment Guarantee Programs: A Survey of Theories and Policy Experiences. *Levy Economics Institute Working Paper,* No. 498, May, www.levy.org

Keynes, John. M. K (1936). *The General Theory of Employment Interest and Money.* London: Palgrave Macmillan.

Kregel, J. (2006). ELR as An Alternative Development Strategy. Mimeo presented at the Jerome Levy Economics Institute conference on Employment Guarantee Policies, October.

Papola, T. S. (2006). Employment Trends in India. In Kaushik Basu (ed.) *The Oxford Companion to Economics in India.* Oxford: Oxford University Press pp. 131–136.

Robeyns, I. (2005). The Capability Approach: A Theoretical Survey. *Journal of Human Development,* Vol. 6, No. 1, pp. 93–114.

Robeyns, I. (2006). The Capability Approach in Practice. *The Journal of Political Philosophy,* Vol. 14, No. 3, pp. 351–376.

Sehnbrunch, K. (2004). From the Quantity of Employment to the Quality of Employment: An Application of the Capability Approach to the Chilean Labor Market. *Center for Latin American Studies University of California, Berkley Working Paper no. 9,* May.

Sen, A. (1981). *Poverty and Famines: An Essay on Entitlement and Deprivation.* Oxford: Clarendon Press.

Sen, A (1993). Capability and Well Being. In M. Nussbaum and A. Sen (eds) *The Quality of Life.* Oxford: Oxford University Press pp. 9–29.

Sen, A. (1997). What's the Points of a Development Strategy? *United Nations Committee on Development and Management of the Market Economy.*

Retrieved from http://eprints.lse.ac.uk/6705/1/What%27s_the_Point_of_a_Development_Strategy.pdf

Sen, A (1997a). *Penalties of Unemployment.* Roma: Temi di discussione del Servizio Studi.

Sen, A. (1997b). Inequality, Unemployment and Contemporary Europe. *International Labor Review*, Vol. 136, No. 2. pp. 155–171.

Sen, A. (1997c). From Income Inequality to Economic Inequality. *Southern Economic Journal*, Vol. 64, No. 2 pp. 384–401.

Sen, A (1999). *Development as Freedom.* Oxford University Press: Oxford.

Sen, A. (2004). Capabilities, Lists, and Public Reason: Continuing the Conversation. *Feminist Economics*, Vol. 10, No. 3, pp. 77–80.

Sharma, A. (2010). Rights-based Legal Guarantee as Development Policy: The Mahatma Gandhi National Rural Employment Guarantee Act. *UNDP India*, Discussion Paper.

Walsh, V. (1995). Amartya Sen on Inequality, Capabilities and Needs. *Science and Society*, Winter 1995; Vol. 59, No. 4, pp 556–569.

Wray, L. R (2007). The Employer of the Last Resort Program: Could It Work for Developing Countries? *Economic and Labour Market Papers*, International Labour Organization.

Wray, L. R. (1998). *Understanding Modern Money: The Key to Full Employment and Price Stability.* Northampton, Mass: Edward Elgar.

Wray, L. R. and Forstater, M. (2004). Full Employment and Economic Justice. In D. Champlin and J. Knoedler (eds.) *The Institutionalist Tradition in Labor Economics.* Armonk: NY: M.E. Sharpe.

Unterhalter, E. (2003). Education, Capabilities and Social Justice, "Paper Commissioned for the *EFA Global Monitoring Report 2003/4, The Leap to Equality.*"

CHAPTER 5

The State, Employer of Last Resort, and Youth Employment: A Case Study of the National Youth Employment Program in Ghana

Richard B. Dadzie

Since independence in 1957, the Ghanaian state's role in employment creation and economic development has followed a dichotomous pattern of heavy or limited state involvement. Heavy state involvement occurred mostly in the period circa independence. The charisma of Kwame Nkrumah and his government allowed for the pursuit of several large government-sponsored projects such as the Volta Dam, which had immense implications for job creation. This project, along with several infrastructure projects in education, roads, and industry, created many jobs and the Ghanaian economy experienced some of its fastest rates of growth and social development in the past five decades. In the period 1966–1981, coup d'états changed the political landscape of the country and even though heavy state intervention was common it was largely not of a developmental nature. Such involvement can be characterized as being akin to the predatory state typology of Evans (1995). Attempts to return the Ghanaian state to democratic principles and stable governments in 1969–1970 and 1979–1981 failed. The failure of these efforts derailed hopes of returning to the earlier period where the state engaged civil society in ways that helped create jobs and promote economic development initiatives. Growth rates in this period of coup d'états were abysmal. Employment stagnated, emigration increased, and the prospects of development were at a standstill.

The era of coup d'états and the associated negative role of the government coincided with trends in West Africa and sub-Saharan Africa (SSA). The growing negative view of government (albeit military) was an important precursor to a new pattern of limited government. In Ghana, the growing distaste for repressive military regimes coincided with the neoclassical counterrevolution and market fundamentalist movement of the 1980s. In developing countries like Ghana, this counterrevolution meant the dismantling of public ownership, development planning, and other forms of state intervention. The state was branded a demon that only took and destroyed, and enriched a few. Within the context of the time, this argument was persuasive. Suggesting that the state was synonymous with declining growth and social decay was something rooted in the experiences of many. Further, arguing that the removal of the state and the installation of market principles in all spheres of life were necessary was a no-brainer. The neoclassical takeover of the two most important agencies responsible for international development and finance (the World Bank and the International Monetary Fund) cemented this new view and led to the adoption of Structural Adjustment Programs (SAPs) in Ghana and elsewhere in SSA by late 1980 (Todaro and Smith, 2012, p. 127). Limited government was the central policy of the SAPs. The SAPs promised two important things. First, they represented a departure from repressive militaristic regimes and, second, they promised accelerated employment generating economic growth, development, and jobs if and only if adjusting nations fully embraced free market principles embedded in the policy prescriptions.

Since the failure of the SAPs (SAPRIN, 2004), limited forms of government intervention in policy initiatives geared toward job creation and economic development have been allowed. In this new era of what Fine and Jomo KS (2006) describes as the Post-Washington Consensus (PWC), state intervention has been allowed in areas such as youth employment. The inability of the SAPs to deliver on the promise of sustainable growth enhancing employment has led many nations to pursue within the so-called Poverty Reduction Strategy Papers (PRSPs) employment programs best suited for their countries. In the West African subregion, these programs have focused on the youth because of the following important reasons. First, youth unemployment has become a security issue given the incidence of child soldiers in the civil wars of Liberia and Sierra Leone. Second, demographic indicators show that the number of youth will continue to increase and, finally, youth employment can contribute to economic development (UNOWA, 2005; ILO-YEN; Ministry of Manpower, Youth and Employment, 2005).

Ghana's National Youth Employment Programme (NYEP) is one such initiative aimed at addressing unemployment issues facing the youth. This chapter will focus on this program and situate the discussion within the context of the role of the state in employment creating economic development. This is an emergent issue in SSA and many policymakers and scholars have recently become enamored with the role of the state in employment creation and economic development (UNOWA, 2005; UNCTAD, 2007; UNECA, 2011). The remainder of this chapter is divided into four sections. The first outlines the problem of youth unemployment in Ghana. The second discusses the history of policy intervention with regard to youth employment and discusses the types and roles of states necessary for the success of interventions such as the NYEP. The third delves into Ghana's NYEP by assessing its structure, achievements, and challenges as well as the ways in which it fits the Employer of Last Resort (ELR) typology described in the second section. The fourth concludes the chapter by highlighting the need for bolder action on job programs such as NYEP as well alternative ways of thinking that acknowledge that for successful jobs programs, states must become developmental, entrepreneurs, and employers of last resort.

Youth Unemployment in Ghana: Understanding the Problem

Given the absence of reliable data on unemployment, what is generally accepted is that a very high proportion of the estimated 8 million youth (ages 15–35) are unemployed or severely underemployed (Ministry of Manpower, Youth and Employment, 2005). Limited data reported by the World Bank estimated youth unemployment rate at 16.6 percent in 2000 (World Development Indicators Online). The reliability of this data is doubtful but it is generally observable that a very high proportion of the youth are unemployed or underemployed in both rural and urban areas. Travel to the two major cities of Accra and Kumasi supports this assertion. This dire situation has resulted because of several factors including (1) the lack of a coherent national development and employment policy, (2) the stagnation of industrial activity since the late 1960s, (3) the reduction of the public sector coupled with the anemic growth of the private sector during the SAPs, and (4) incoherent and inconsistent educational systems ill-suited for important sectors of the economy such as agriculture and industry.

Unemployment among youth with tertiary education is phenomenal. "Everyone wants to work in one of the banks in Accra, even those with degrees unrelated to finance such as chemical engineering" (Interview with Deputy-General Secretary, Public Sector Workers Union of Ghana Trade Union Congress). Youth with secondary and/or primary education face an even more difficult situation. Many in this group find employment in menial occupations including "trotro" (private bus) mates and garden boys. Occupations available for youth in this category are largely unstable and have very poor working conditions. Gender dimensions of youth unemployment are also evident across Ghana. Young men tend to engage in those employments with relatively higher wages or potential for higher wages and young women are employed in petty trading and other relatively low-wage occupations.

Youth unemployment in Ghana has not spilled into the political-security sphere as it did in Sierra Leone and Liberia; however, among the several socioeconomic issues that have emerged as a result of poor employment conditions is emigration or "brain drain." An estimated 60 percent of graduates from the University of Ghana Medical School have emigrated. Occupations such as nursing have also experienced similar trends. For example, for nurses applying for nursing work permits to the United Kingdom, Ghanaian nurses rank in the top ten and the United Kingdom remains the favorite destination for nearly 80 percent of all Ghanaian nurses emigrating (Dovlo, 2004).

The Role of the State in Employment Generation: History of Policy Intervention for Youth Employment in Ghana and the Need for an Aggressive Alternative

In the era of SAPs, an important policy intervention that affected the youth was the 1987 educational reform. This reform was marked by a significant reduction in the duration of preuniversity education as the government was forced to make several budget cuts in sectors including basic and tertiary education. Technical and vocational education was promoted in an attempt to produce graduates who were more employable in those areas such as agriculture considered necessary for national development. The logic was that many of these graduates would help exploit the country's comparative advantages and be labor market ready. The results of the 1987 reform have been largely negative since the Government of Ghana (GoG) has altered the system more than once. The overwhelming majority of scholars have argued that the reform had negative outcomes since youth unemployment worsened as aggregate demand fell because of the reduction of government budgets. Also, many have argued that the quality of education fell since many teachers saw real reductions in their income (SAPRIN, 2004).

In the era of PWC, limited forms of intervention have been allowed under the PRSPs. Ghana has attempted various long-term economic development plans that have had as cornerstones various attempts to create national employment policies targeting the youth. The "Vision 2020" plan adopted in 1996 had as one of its core goals the enhancement of the employability of youth through various training programs. The employment policy of "Vision 2020" was never implemented in any serious manner. Since 2000, two PRSPs have been developed as part of debt relief packages associated with the Heavily Indebted Poor Countries initiative. PRSP-I was implemented from 2001 to 2005. One of the policy interventions of relevance to the youth was the introduction of entrepreneurial programs at the tertiary level especially in agricultural colleges. The goal was to help young graduates identify and initiate various agriculture-related investment projects. PRSP-II was implemented from 2006 to 2009. Under this strategy paper, tax incentives were designed to incentivize various corporations to hire new graduates from the growing number of universities. Project-specific interventions such as the National Mass Cocoa Spraying Programme and National Forest Plantation Programme were all enacted under the PRSPs to create jobs particularly for the youth but all these initiatives have yielded limited results. A significant problem under the various programs has been poor monitoring, documentation, and evaluation. The PRSPs-inspired employment initiatives have suffered the plight of their cousin, the SAPs. They have failed to generate employment particularly for the youth (Otoo & Torgbe, 2011).

In the context of the above discussion, it is clear that addressing youth employment requires renewed roles for the state that put it beyond the "minimalist" state enacted under SAPs and PRSPs. An active state committed to bold initiatives can resolve the demand-side problem, which appears to dampen the prospects of employment for the youth. A developmental state that fulfills its duties as an entrepreneur of last resort and an ELR in the strongest possible way is necessary if youth unemployment is to be seriously tackled.

Developmental State

The notion that the state has an important role to play in employment generation and economic development can be traced back to the origins of capitalism, particularly during the mercantile period (Reinert, 1999). In the recent period, Johnson (1982) is credited with formalizing the concept of the developmental state after his careful analyses of the exceptional role the state played in the development of Japan after World War II (Cumings, 1999, 63). Onis (1991) advanced and refined the concept by arguing that "the logic of developmental state rests precisely on the combination of bureaucratic autonomy with an unusual degree of public-private cooperation" (p. 115). And Castells (1992) provided a concrete definition of the developmental state when he argued that

> a state is developmental when it establishes as its principle of legitimacy, its ability to promote and sustain development, understanding by development the combination of steady high rates of economic growth and structural change in the productive system, both domestically and its relationship to the international economy. (p. 56)

As a concept, the developmental state has been described as antiorthodox economics and passé (Hollerman, 1983; Yamamura, 1983; Beason & Weinstein, 1995). It has been accepted as different but nonaltering of neoclassical economic theory, which is evident in the SAPs and PWC. In spite of the staunch critique and rejection of the developmental state paradigm, it has remained a powerful alternative as many scholars have worked to improve our understanding of its central tenets (Amsden, 1989; Wade, 1990; Evans, 1995; Stein, 1996; Chang, 2007; Reinert, 1999; Mkandawire, 2001; Kohli, 2004; Fine and Jomo, 2006; Khan, 2007).

Scholars of the developmental state paradigm have identified the following as its most important attributes. First, a developmental state is consistent in its pursuit of developmental objectives and it is committed to those objectives. Failure in achieving developmental objectives does not mean an abandoning of those objectives altogether. Second, the developmental state is an activist state. The state is not relegated to the role of an overseer. The developmental state evolves as the needs of the society in which it is embedded change. Change is welcomed so long as it does not detract from the overall development objective. Third, the developmental state uses trade and FDI policies in such a way as to promote domestic productive capacity and technological learning. Finally, the developmental state is well-staffed, risk-taking, socially legitimate and democratic. The goals of the developmental state are numerous and include employment, industrialization, poverty reduction, and access to healthcare.

Entrepreneur of Last Resort

In order to act as an entrepreneur of last resort, the state must invoke what Evans (1995) refers to as the demiurge role of the state. In this role, the state becomes directly involved in the production activities through direct production and employment. The states' involvement may be complementary to that of the private sector; however, it is mostly a replacement of and an injection into an area of the economy where private capital is inadequate in resolving those issues identified by the state as necessary for national development (Evans, 1995, p. 79). In the past, in many developing nations including Ghana, state-owned enterprises were the embodiment of the demiurge role, but in the absence of the state's embedded autonomy,[1] the execution of this has been lackluster.

Amsden (1989) provides an excellent example of an effective execution of the demiurge role of the state, which makes it an entrepreneur of last resort. Using the creation of the Pohang Iron and Steel Company[2] as an example, she showed one way in which the government can act as an entrepreneur in a positive way. Other heterodox scholars of development such as Chang (2007) and Reinert (1999) have shown that the history of now industrialized economies around the world is strewn with several instances of the state acting as an entrepreneur of last resort. Cipolla (1970) presents further convincing evidence from the economic history of Western Europe. In his analysis of the economic decline of empires, he showed how Dukes and other state officials in Northern Italy acted as entrepreneurs of last resort to sustain the declining silk industry and upgrade industrial capacities in other manufacturing sectors. These examples point to the fact that when all else fails, the state's ability to engender growth cannot be underestimated.

Employer of Last Resort or Public Service Employment

Within the context of SSA, the notion of the state serving as an ELR is not new. Pan-Africanists like Ghana's Kwame Nkrumah argued for this in the early 1960s. Pan-Africanist and scholar of African history Cheikh Anta Diop (1974) also argued strongly for the pursuit of full employment across SSA. In his 14 steps to African unity, he argued that successful industrialization and development in SSA will depend on the ability "to carry out with conviction a policy of full employment" (p. 89). Around the rest of world, economists of the heterodox persuasion have been ardent supporters of the notion of the state as an ELR (Copeland, 1967; Minsky, 1986; Gordon, 1997; Wray, 1998; Forstater, 1999; Kaboub, 2006, 2007). It is important to note that within neoclassical economic theory, the concept of the state acting as an ELR is nonsensical from two viewpoints. First, the labor market clears and all unemployment is transitory and more seriously unemployment is a voluntary choice given the options between work and leisure that face the rational individual. Second, government failures are bound to occur; therefore, if the state is allowed into the business of allocating an important resource such as labor, only perverse outcomes await.

Minsky (1986) is credited with reviving the concept of the state as an ELR. Wray (1998) clarified and expanded the concept and Kaboub (2006) has shown its applicability in developing nations. Drawing on the insights of these scholars, a state acting as an ELR will (1) create demand for labor at a floor or minimum wage, which is independent of business profit expectations (Minsky, 1986, Kaboub, 2007), (2) guarantee a real job opportunity to anyone willing and able to work (Wray, 1998), (3) serve as a complement rather than a substitute to private-sector jobs (Wray, 1998), and (4) be a decentralized program financed by the government[3] (Wray, 1998; Kaboub, 2007). In its current form, the ELR has two important characteristics that make it extremely promising. First, it is countercyclical in that during recessions, workers in the program will grow as they are displaced from private-sector employment. During an expansion, workers in the program will decline, since private-sector employment will be readily available. Second, cost estimates particularly within the context of developing countries show that spending for the program can be financed with less than 5 percent of GDP (Kaboub, 2007, p. 497).

Ghana's National Youth Employment Programme: Structure, Achievements, and Challenges

Ghana's NYEP is an important attempt by the GoG to effectively address youth unemployment. The program is an attempt by the state to serve as an ELR. Even though this is a step in the direction, the success of the program depends on the ability of the GoG to achieve developmental state status and act in ways that make it an entrepreneur of last resort. The NYEP in its current state does not go far enough to address the existing problem and contrary to the notion of the World Bank (2009), it is not too expensive when the potential future losses to economic growth and development are considered; also, a rural works program that is deemed more cost-effective and thus efficient can be subsumed under a broader public-sector employment program such as the NYEP.

NYEP: Structure, Achievements, and Challenges

The NYEP emerged out of a milieu of ideas and attempts to address youth unemployment including The Skills Training Employment Placement (STEP) program, the National Youth Fund (NYF), and various schemes under the Kuffour government's Presidents' Special Initiative program. Many of these emerged in the early 2000s and were influential in the creation of the relatively bolder NYEP. Planning for the NYEP occurred in 2005 and the program took full effect in 2006. The overall objective of the program is to empower the youth to contribute meaningfully to economic development through various jobs. Specific goals included controlling rural-urban migration by ensuring that employment opportunities are created nationwide and creating opportunities for self-employment ventures. Initial employment targets were 175,000 jobs by the end of the first year (2006–2007) and 500,000 jobs in three years (2006–2009). As of 2010, the program had successfully employed 300,000 youth. Jobs in the program occur in modules in areas such as agribusiness, waste and sanitation, information and communication technology, teaching, and health. Ten modules were implemented from 2006 to 2009 with an additional four modules[4] added since September 2010.

The implementation of the modules is decentralized to ensure that certain modules have more relevance in particular districts (county equivalents) across the country. The Ministry of Manpower, Youth and Employment oversees the implementation of the NYEP through a national coordinator, a variety of national deputies for operational areas such as finance, 10 regional (state equivalent) coordinators, and 197 district-level coordinators.[5] In executing each module, submodules determine the specific activities that participants perform. As an example, in the community education teaching assistants' module, participants can be involved in one of three submodules: basic classroom instruction, refresher courses instruction, and adult literacy. Activities in these submodules include preschool care, assistance in preparing for professional

Table 5.1 Selected modules and levels of employment, 2010

Modules	*Employment*
Community teaching assistants	17,674
Community policing assistants	3,457
Health extension workers	12,592
Youth in waste and sanitation	23,528
Youth in road maintenance and repairs	11,261

Source: Public Sector Workers Union, Ghana Trade Union Congress.

examinations and night classes for working adults (Ministry of Manpower, Youth and Employment, 2005). Table 5.1 shows estimated employment levels in the top five modules in 2010. Thus far, over 2,000 schools have been revamped under the program in rural areas across the country, and cities like Accra and Kumasi look relatively cleaner mostly because of the waste and sanitation module. Participants receive a monthly wage of 50 Ghana Cedis (GhC) (an estimated US$30 in February 2012), which is far below the minimum wage of civil service workers (Baah et al., 2009).

The NYEP has several important characteristics that qualify it as an ELR program. At first glance, the NYEP meets the ELR criterion because it (1) has created a demand for youth workers at a minimum monthly wage, (2) guarantees a job in one of the 14 modules for registered youths albeit for a maximum of two years, (3) complements other private-sector jobs in areas such as waste and sanitation,[6] hairdressing, mobile phone repairs, and assembly, and finally, (4) is a decentralized program funded 100 percent by the GoG. A second and deeper look reveals important challenges that undermine the program's ability to be a true ELR program. Three main challenges can be identified. First, the nature of jobs and the working conditions do not encourage participation from certain sections of the youth population particularly those with tertiary education. Most participants are employed under informal arrangements without employment contracts and do not have access to social security, healthcare, and paid annual leave. Further, payment of the monthly allowance (which is far below minimum monthly wages in the country) is on an irregular schedule and it is not uncommon to have allowances delayed by several weeks. Work days often involve overtime work, which is not compensated. These working conditions have made the program unattractive for youth with higher levels of education.

Second, the current structure of the program makes it a stopgap measure with no effective exit plan to ensure permanent employment of youth who have participated in the various modules. Currently, there is a maximum of two years of employment under the program. As envisioned in the formulation of the program, there was to be an exit plan that ensured a smooth transition from the NYEP into permanent employment either in the government or in the private sector. For example, youth who exhaust two years in the Community Policing Assistants or Health Extension Workers modules were to be transitioned into employment with the Ghana Police and Ghana Health Service. Unfortunately, the execution of the exit plan has been a failure and virtually all participants who exit the program remain unemployed. The failure of these exit plans prompted the addition of new modules such as Youth in Dressmaking that could encourage self-employment. The absence of a strong government with active demand management policies can be blamed for the ineffective exit plans.

Third, coordination of the program is very poor. Irregular funding often hampers the success of skills training and recruiting efforts. Coordination with other youth-oriented programs such as the National Service Scheme (NSS) is also very poor. The NSS is mandated by law to target university graduates and requires one year of service to the country in various areas including teaching in remote communities for the GoG or working for firms in the private sector but with salaries paid by the NSS. As it currently stands the NSS and NYEP are separate initiatives with similar goals. The impression in Ghana is that the NSS is for the educated and NYEP is for all other youth. Better coordination of both initiatives within the context of an ELR program will go a long way in making the NYEP more effective. As part of coordination, evaluation procedures within the program must be revisited to address these challenges particularly that of the exit plan.

Conclusions and Policy Recommendations

As Ghana continues to work toward developing its economy, addressing the youth unemployment problem will continue to be central to the ability of the country to achieve its development objectives. The ability of the state to create, sustain, and ensure the success of programs such as the NYEP depends on the extent to which the state is prepared to deviate from decades of neoliberal-inspired policies and accept heterodox-inspired policies that call for the state to become developmental and execute its functions as an entrepreneur of last resort and an ELR.

The NYEP is a step in the right direction. Some success has been achieved and the potential of greater success remains if bold steps are taken. Four such bold steps are (1) outright rejection of the notion that government intervention in the labor market leads to government failure, (2) pursuit of a national employment program that meets in the strictest terms the tenets of ELR by guaranteeing a job to anyone (not just youth) who is willing and able to work at a livable wage, (3) development of a national industrial policy that has at its core the integration of the youth, and (4) development of a national development strategy that ensures beneficial engagement with economic powers around the world. Pursuing these recommendations will ensure that the Ghanaian state can act as an entrepreneur of last resort, ELR, and a developmental state.

Rejecting outright neoclassical-inspired labor market conclusions is important because as Keynes showed the problem of unemployment is not a choice-theoretic decision by rational economic agents. Unemployment is an inherent feature of capitalism that must be actively addressed. A recent publication by the World Bank (2009) suggested that the NYEP is simply too expensive and that it should be scaled back if Ghana does not want to compromise its potential for economic growth and development. Embedded in this argument is the belief that the government's role in improving labor market conditions is limited and deleterious. Furthermore, in this publication, it is argued that in the utmost situation that the government must intervene, it must do so in rural areas because that is where the greatest potential to impact the economy lies given the agricultural resources there. This report fails to recognize that youth unemployment is unbiased toward urban and rural areas and, furthermore, that Ghana is becoming more urban and addressing these issues on a national scale requires a strong national effort such as the NYEP. Furthermore, it fails to recognize, as has been shown by several heterodox economists, that a sovereign country such as Ghana that is the sole issuer of its own currency is faced with very little restrictions in its ability to fund a program such as the NYEP (Wray, 1998; Kaboub, 2007). The conclusions of this World Bank publication underscore the continued dominance of perpetuation of the notion that the state is always an inhibitor rather than a promoter of good. In order to seriously attack the youth unemployment issue, such thinking must be done away with outright.

An ELR-type program, such as the NYEP, is essential for the economic development of Ghana. The potential of this program to generate income and stimulate spending requires that a national jobs program be pursued. This jobs program must be open to everyone in the labor force (not just the youth) who are willing and able to work, and such work must be compensated at a minimum livable wage. Such a program will increase the number of potential workers and increase the productive capacity of Ghana in areas such as agroindustry especially if the GoG serves as an entrepreneur of last resort by acting out its demiurge role. Sociologically, such a bold program will ensure that all Ghanaians including the youth feel empowered and feel that they are contributing to the development of their country.

As has been shown by industrialized countries including newcomers from East Asia, industrial policy creation is an important step to successful economic growth, development, and employment generation. Integrating all Ghanaians in an industrial policy program and particularly the youth has the potential to yield very positive rewards. Such rewards could include a job, a sense of self-worth and accomplishment, and a much developed country in which to grow old and raise a family. Developing such an industrial policy will require a developmental state that acts as an entrepreneur of last resort in areas where private capital is simply inadequate. For example, the state could spearhead agroprocessing in regions such as the Central Region where citrus production is fast growing but citrus processing is still anemic. A state acting as an entrepreneur of last resort can generate employment in areas such as health and information, communication, and technology where many Ghanaians overseas have strong expertise. Alice Amsden (at the African Programme on Rethinking Development Economics, Johannesburg, South Africa, May 2011) argued that the state can pursue reverse brain drain to attract those talents that citizens of their country may have but are using elsewhere in the world through the creation of employment initiatives that guarantee good wages and excellent working conditions. To seriously address youth unemployment and unemployment in general, the state in the performance of its ELR duties can integrate the youth in industrial policy planning and attract citizens who reside elsewhere in the world back into the country with guaranteed jobs tied to the nation's development project.

Finally, the execution of bolder steps that go beyond the NYEP discussed above must recognize the reality of the global political economy of today. As is already the case, new global powers such as China and India are having tremendous impact in Ghana and elsewhere in SSA.

A bold step requiring bolder action from the state will be necessary to ensure, either alone or with other nations in SSA, that investments and production in Ghana have terms that are job generating for the youth and all citizens. Such terms could include local content requirements, significant Ghanaian involvement in projects such as road building, and so on. Heterodox development economists have shown that the process of learning for development is enhanced when such terms are demanded and enforced. In the process of learning, new employment is generated and the potential of reducing unemployment is enhanced (Khan, 2007).

To achieve the true potential of a jobs program such as the NYEP and to achieve growth and development it is incumbent upon the state to act in a way that is theoretically in contradistinction to the neoclassical paradigm. States must actively engage their societies in ways that allow them to achieve embedded autonomy. Achieving this requires that states be bolder in the methods in which they adopt to address issues such as youth unemployment. Ghana's NYEP is one such important attempt and its success now and in the future will depend on how boldly the Ghanaian state acts.

Acknowledgments

The author gratefully acknowledges the comments and help of Bernard Adjei who is the Deputy Secretary-General of the Public Sector Workers Union of Ghana's Trade Union Congress.

Notes

1. Embedded implies a concrete set of links that connect the state to important social groups with whom the state shares a joint project of transformation. Autonomy refers to the state's ability to provide institutionalized channels for the continuous negotiation and renegotiation of goals and policies (Evans, 1995, p. 59).
2. In the 1970s and 1980s, Pohang Steel and Iron Company POSCO became one of the largest producers of steel products in the world and surpassed all of the steel producers in the United States. POSCO benchmarked and borrowed production technologies from Nippon Steel in Japan. Further, POSCO was able to capture over half of the market share for imported steel from Japan. The Kwangyang Steel plant also made tremendous strides in making Korean one of the world's leading producers of steel products (Amsden, 1989, pp. 293–297). Kwan S. Kim (1995) argued that Korea's development success

was brought forth by a neo-mercantilist model that was characterized by a series of government interventions that went beyond the minimalist advocated by neoclassical and market-oriented economists.

3. Proponents of public-sector employment argue that any sovereign government has the financial ability to pay for an ELR program. This notion builds on Abba Lerner's Functional Finance theory.
4. The 14 modules are Community Education Teaching Assistants, Community Policing Assistants, Health Extension Workers, Youth in Waste and Sanitation (operated by Zoomlion Ghana Ltd.), Paid Interns, Youth in Mobile Phone Repairs and Assembling, Basket Weaving, Youth in Dressmaking, Youth in Film Making, Aviation Security, Youth in Road Maintenance and Repairs, Youth in Hairdressing, Youth in Bamboo Processing, and Youth in Prisons Service Assistants.
5. The program is funded through the Ghana Education Trust Fund, National Health Insurance Authority, Communication Service Tax, Ministry of Finance and Economic Planning, Road Fund and District Assembly Common Fund. As discussed earlier, under Abba Lerner's functional finance and Wray's (1998) modern money perspective, funding for the program should not be an impediment and, as Kaboub (2006) showed, developing countries are just as capable of implementing such initiatives.
6. This module is run in partnership with Zoomlion Ghana Limited, a private waste management enterprise in Ghana.

Bibliography

Amsden, A. (1989). *Asia's Next Giant: South Korea and Late Industrialization.* Oxford University Press.

Baah, A. Y., Achakoma, K., & Ampratwum, E. (2009). *Working Conditions in the National Youth Employment Programme in Ghana.* Accra: Ghana TUC/FES.

Bank, W. (2009). *Ghana Job Creation and Skills Development.* Washington, D.C.: World Bank.

Beason, R. & Weinstein, D. (1995). The MITI Myth. *American Enterprise,* 6(4): 84. Retrieved October 18, 2010, from EBSCO.

Castells, M. (1992). Four Asian Tigers with a Dragon Head. In Richard P. Appelbaum and Jeffrey Henderson (eds), *States and Development in the Asian Pacific Rim* (pp. 33–70). Newbury Park, CA: Sage Publications.

Chang, Ha-Joon. (2007). *Institutional Change and Economic Development.* Tokyo: United Nations University Press.

Cipolla, C. M. (1970). *The Economic Decline of Empires.* London: The Camelot Press Ltd.

Copeland, M. A. (1967). Implementing the Objective of Full Employment in Our Free Enterprise Economy. In C. C. Thompson (ed.), *Institutional*

Adjustment: A Challenge to a Changing Economy. Austin, TX: University of Texas Press.

Cumings, B. (1999). Webs with No Spiders, Spiders with No Webs: The Genealogy of the Developmental State. In M. Woo-Cumings (ed.), *The Developmental State* (pp. 61–92). Ithaca: Cornell University Press.

Diop, C. A. (1974). *Black Africa: The Economic and Cultural Basis for a Federated State.* Westport, CT: Lawrence Hill & Company.

Dovlo, D. (2004). The Brain Drain in Africa: Am Emerging Challenge to Health Professionals' Education. *Journal of Higher Education in Africa,* 2(3): 1–18.

Evans, P. (1995). *Embedded Autonomy: States & Industrial Transformation.* Princeton, NJ: Princeton University Press.

Fine, B., & Jomo, K. S. (2006). *The New Development Economics after the Washington Consensus.* New York: Zed Books.

Forstater, M. (1999). Functional Finance and Full Employment: Lessons from Lerner for Today. *Journal of Economic Issues,* 33(2): 475–482.

Gordon, W. C. (1997). Job Assurance: The Job Guarantee Revisited. *Journal of Economic Issues,* 21(3): 817–825.

Hollerman, L. (1983). Review of MITI and the Japanese Miracle by Chalmers Johnson. *Journal of Asian Studies,* 42(2): 414–415.

Johnson, C. (1982). *MITI and the Japanese Miracle: The Growth of Industrial Policy, 1925–1975.* Stanford, CA: Stanford University Press.

Kaboub, F. (2006). *A Roadmap to Full Employment and Price Stability: The Case of Tunisia.* Ph.D. Dissertation, University of Missouri-Kansas City.

Kaboub, F. (2007). Institutional Adjustment Planning for Full Employment. *Journal of Economic Issues,* 41(2): 495–502.

Khan, M. (2007). Governance, Economic Growth and Development since the 1960s. In J. A. Ocampo, K. S. Joma, & R. Vos (eds), *Growth Divergences: Explaining Differences in Economic Performance* (pp. 285–323). New York: Zed Books.

Kohli, A. (2004). *State-Directed: Political Power and Industrialization in the Global Periphery.* New York: Cambridge University Press.

Ministry of Manpower, Youth and Employment: Government of Ghana. (2005). *Youth Employment Implementation Guidelines.* Accra: Ministry of Manpower, Youth and Employment.

Minsky, Hyman. P. (1986). *Stabilizing an Unstable Economy.* New Haven, CT: Yale University Press.

Mkandawire, T. (2001). Thinking about Developmental States in Africa. *Cambridge Journal of Economics,* 25(3): 289–313.

Onis, Z. (1991). The Logic of the Developmental State. *Comparative Politics,* 24(1): 109–126.

Otoo, K. N. & Torgbe, M. (2011). *National Initiatives on Youth Employment in Ghana.* Accra: Labour Research and Policy Institute, Ghana Trade Union Congress.

Reinert, E. (1999). The Role of the State in Economic Growth. *Journal of Economic Studies,* 26 (4-5): 268–326.

SAPRIN. (2004). *Structural Adjustment: The Policy Roots of Economic Crisis, Poverty and Inequality.* New York: Zed Books.

Stein, H. (1996). *Asian Industrialization and Africa: Studies in Policy Alternatives for Structural Adjustment.* New York: St. Martins Press.

Todaro, M. & Smith, S. (2012). *Economic Development.* Essex, UK: Pearson.

UNCTAD. (2007). *Reclaiming Policy Space: Domestic Resource Mobilization and Developmental States.* New York: United Nations.

UNECA. (2011). *Governing Development in Africa—The Role of the State in Economic Transformation.* Addis Ababa: United Nations Economic Commission for Africa.

UNOWA. (2005). *Youth Unemployment and Regional Insecurity in West Africa.* Dakar: United Nations Office for West Africa.

Wade, R. (1990). *Governing the Market: Economic Theory and the Role of Government in East Asian Industrialization.* Princeton, NJ: Princeton University Press.

Wray, L. Randall. (1998). *Understanding Modern Money: The Key to Full Employment and Price Stability.* Northampton, MA: Edward Elgar.

Yamamura, K. (1983). Review of MITI and the Japanse Miracle by Chalmers Johnson. *Journal of Japanese Studies,* 9(2): 211.

CHAPTER 6

The Job Guarantee and Municipal Confederalism: Exploring the National and Local Levels of Program Operation

Mathew Forstater

In recent years, an approach to full employment known alternatively as Employer of Last Resort (ELR), Job Guarantee (JG), and Public Service Employment (PSE) has been put forward as an effective strategy for eliminating involuntary unemployment and promoting economic stability. It has also been argued that JG may be used to promote environmental sustainability and, more generally, as a vehicle for progressive social policies (Forstater, 2004). Most of the recent proposals for a JG have been put forward within what has come to be known as Modern Monetary Theory (MMT), a term that encompasses the Chartalist approach to money and the functional finance approach to managing government budgets (Wray, 1998).

The challenge for the JG policy approach is to find the right balance between the national and local levels of its political operation. On the one hand, modern money and functional finance require that the program be paid for at the federal level, but, on the other hand, most proposals have program management and organization conducted at the local level by NGOs (nongovernmental organizations) and local governments. This chapter outlines the ways in which the communitarian anarchist and social ecology notion of "municipal confederalism" presents possibilities for an appropriate mix of regional and local aspects of JG, along with other advantages of the municipal confederalist framework (and anarchism generally), including opening up spaces for noncapitalist social relations of production.

The Job Guarantee: Basic Outline and Benefits

According to the JG paradigm, government offers a public service job to anyone ready and willing to work, no means tests or time limits. The federal government pays the basic JG wage-benefits package, but community groups, NGOs, nonprofit enterprises, and local governments administer and manage the program. There are always enough jobs to employ everyone who needs one, as government provides an infinitely elastic demand for labor. The program creates a strong countercyclical stabilizer, expanding when the economy goes into a downturn and contracting as the private-sector demand for labor rises.

In addition to providing full employment and macroeconomic stability, and reducing the social and economic costs of unemployment, JG has numerous other potential benefits. Staying employed maintains the skills of workers, whose productivity declines during periods of joblessness. JG can provide training and education that may open opportunities for employment in new occupations and industries. Businesses benefit from hiring workers who have been able to maintain and even enhance their capabilities. By guaranteeing high and stable incomes and demand, the uncertainty characterizing investment decisions is reduced, and firms have the resources and incentives to retool and make use of the latest technologies.

In addition to creating jobs, income, and demand, and developing skills and offering opportunities for training and education, JG also supports the provision of public services. Suddenly there is no labor constraint for providing services often in short supply and for addressing unmet social and community needs. Libraries and community centers can stay open every night, and additional helping hands are available for playgrounds, nursing homes, and recycling centers. Revitalized infrastructure reduces costs and stimulates productivity.

JG is also the only real means of achieving the right to employment found in numerous governmental and other documents, such as the United Nations' "Universal Declaration of Human Rights." The right to employment is also the most important means to many other economic and social rights, such as the rights to food, housing, and healthcare.

While conventional fiscal stimulus is unlikely to provide true full employment or to reconcile full employment and price stability, JG addresses unemployment due to both insufficient effective demand and ongoing structural and technological change. In addition, the JG approach deals with the functionality of unemployment, which is completely unaddressed by traditional Keynesian policies.

JG as a Vehicle for Social Policy

The JG approach to full employment and price stability can also serve as the basis for humanistic social policies. Under such a program, a wide variety of social policies may be introduced that otherwise would not stand a chance. To understand how this might work, consider that workers will always have the option to take a JG job. Now imagine what might happen if the JG wage-benefits package included health insurance. Employers in the private sector would have to match the JG wage benefits, either line by line or in some other compensating way. Private businesses would be compelled by "market" pressures to either offer health insurance or compensate in some alternative way (higher salary, more chance for advancement, other benefits, or some other attractive part of the offer). Likewise, since the JG wage would be the *de facto* minimum wage, increases in the JG wage could also be used to pressure businesses to raise wages (or some other compensating feature of their offer). Consider what might happen if the JG job came with childcare. It is the same with worker health and safety issues, and general job environment. The list of ways in which JG employment might be used as a "benchmark" to increase the quality of private-sector jobs is limited only by imagination.

Next, consider the possibilities offered by millions of new workers available to do public service. Suddenly, there would no longer be any financial or labor constraint to the provision of public and community services (other than the "real" constraints of population size, skills and education, and so on). Habitat for Humanity and Meals on Wheels would always have enough labor, public libraries and community centers could stay open every night, and there would be additional helping hands on playgrounds, at subway stations, in nursing homes, and at recycling centers. The environment benefits would be numerous, from increased cleanup and enhanced parks and recreation to tree planting and the provision of new hiking trails. We know from the history of the New Deal era Works Progress Administration (WPA) in the

United States and other successful public service programs just how productive the contributions can be (we can also learn from the mistakes of such programs—e.g., race and gender discrimination must not be tolerated).

A JG program could also be used to redefine just what constitutes valuable work in our society. Presently, the market is used as the yardstick, so if you cannot make your way in the private sector, your life calling must not be valuable. Under the JG program, society is free to decide what qualifies as a JG job. Musicians and artists might be free to follow their calling. Oral histories can be documented and preserved through interviews with the elderly. Community gardens can thrive, with JG chefs preparing meals. Addressing the historical legacy of patriarchy and gender exploitation, care for one's own children and one's own home can be considered valid JG work. Even education and training may be considered public services.

Private versus Social "Efficiency"

JG activities should not be evaluated according to private-sector efficiency criteria, but by whether they achieve broader social, macroeconomic, and environmental goals. Capitalist firms are compelled by competitive pressures to use cost-minimizing methods of production, regardless of whether such methods are consistent with other societal goals, such as full employment or ecological sustainability. Because they are not for profit, there is a great flexibility in the design of JG activities that are freed from market constraints. For example, more labor-intensive methods may be used even where more capital-intensive methods are available. JG activities and methods may be selected to avoid bottlenecks and structural rigidities associated with high levels of employment and capacity utilization. In pursuing environmental sustainability, JG activities and production methods may be selected so that they do not use exhaustible resources in short supply and so they do not pollute or aggravate other environmental problems. This is independent of whether or not the JG activities perform any explicit environmental service (which of course they can).

It should be becoming clear from the discussion that the JG program has the potential for creating spaces for noncapitalist social relations. Just as JG activities can be designed to pollute less or to use more labor-intensive methods, they can also be designed to be less hierarchical and more egalitarian, with more consensus-based decision making.

Federally funded, Locally administered

If the jobs created through the JG program are to truly serve the community then the community and neighborhood organizations must take the reins and administer the programs to the fullest extent possible, rather than having the federal government involved in the majority of administration. The federal government's job is to provide the wages and benefits. The initial attempt to employ JG workers must be through registered community service organizations that already exist. In this way the program will be able to employ individuals with minimal additional bureaucracy, and will in addition supply labor to organizations that provide needed public and social services that enhance the quality of life in that region. Because the federal government pays the wage-benefits package, community service organizations obtain additional workers at no extra cost. Communities will experience an increase in a variety of public services in their region, and this in turn will contribute to an increased quality of life for all members of the community, especially the less well-off. JG workers themselves must also have the opportunity to initiate and develop public and community service projects:

> We must develop socially useful forms of work, which enhance the creativity and involvement of workers . . .. The most rewarding jobs are those which give opportunities for creativity, provide a living wage and have a beneficial effect. People like to do, and like to be seen to be doing, good works. Our cities provide numerous opportunities for congenial employment, from beautifying our cities with gardens to mending footpaths and building playgrounds . . .. Real job-creation schemes involve the workers in the goals and strategies of the employment. Let us allow people the dignity of being involved in identifying, as well as doing, useful employment.
>
> (Short, 1989, p. 127)

Those involved in the early stages of the drafting of the 1946 Employment Act and the 1978 Humphrey-Hawkins bill in the United States witnessed employment guarantees eliminated from the final legislation. More recently, advocates of the NREGA (National Rural Employment Guarantee Act) in India saw the program limited to 100 days a year, and the Argentine *jefes* program (*Plan Jefes de Hogar*) included only "heads of households" despite supporters at the highest levels of government. History teaches that successful efforts at utilizing governmental institutions are enhanced by pressures stemming from grassroots activism and popular organization (Rose, 1995). Organizing the unemployed, the underemployed, and even the homeless, with employed and unemployed working together, may prove effective (Groff, 1997). Neighborhood and Community Unemployment Councils can play important roles, as they have in the past (Ervin, 1994).

Municipal Confederalism as a Framework for Job Guarantee

Given the important relation of the local and regional levels of the political organization of JG, it is necessary to explore frameworks within which the program can be implemented. One obvious possibility would be that the federal government funds the wages and benefits (and material costs) and state and local governments administer the program. While local governments may play some role, it has already been noted that community and neighborhood organizations, NGOs, and nonprofit enterprises will be the primary institutions employing JG workers, and that workers themselves will have a voice in initiating and organizing the projects. In addition, current political boundaries often make no economic or ecological sense. Thus there is a need to learn from alternative institutional structures. The communal anarchist and social ecology notion of municipal confederalism (also known as libertarian municipalism) provides one possible framework.

Anarchism views large, centralized political and economic activity as problematic in and of itself. Anarchists therefore promote political and economic decentralization. This should not be confused, however, with supporting the creation of isolated self-sustaining localities. Rather, some type of confederation among interdependent communities is required.

For the most part, anarchists adopt the position that—to the extent possible—consumption should be primarily from local production and production should be primarily for local consumption. This reduces many environmental and other social costs and promotes participatory democracy. Environmental science, however, has come a long way since Schumacher's brilliant *Small is Beautiful.* Analysis of the "ecological footprint" of activity has demonstrated that there may be considerable exceptions to strict localism.

A similar perspective is necessary regarding the scale of productive activity. Anarchists see that there might be situations where economies of scale may be beneficial, but they also see many diseconomies involved in overcentralized industrialization. Anarchists view most present political units as too large, and even those that are not oversized often have boundaries that make no economic or ecological sense. In this they are guided by bioregionalism, which sees the natural political and economic unit as an ecological one (Milani, 2000). There are many issues that require coordination and cooperation among communities. Municipal confederalism recognizes that interdependence remains crucial, even among otherwise self-sustaining bioregions (Bookchin, 1993).

Anarchists use municipal confederalism as the basis for alternative economic planning. Municipal confederalism makes an important distinction between policymaking and the execution of policies. Policymaking is based on the local community assemblies practicing participatory democracy, but administration and coordination are the responsibility of confederal councils (see Hawkins, 1993).

Anarchists have paid particular attention to issues regarding the division of labor. They oppose the division between manual and intellectual labor, claiming that all society's members need the opportunity to engage in both physical and mental work (Kropotkin, 1974). In addition, anarchists oppose the division between the "field" and the "workshop," again proposing that all individuals require the chance to operate in both settings. There is a great potential for this type of approach within the framework of JG. There is no reason JG workers should be confined to a single activity or employment, not even the most common objection that it decreases productivity, since the benefits of specialization can be had without the negative effects on workers by employing a division of tasks while permitting individuals to alternate between the various assignments.

Anarchists pay close attention to the role of work in human development. In this they take something of an anthropological view of work as an integral part of human existence. As Schumacher, whose work Roszak states "belongs to that subterranean tradition of organic and decentralist economics whose major spokesmen include Prince Kropotkin" (Roszak, 1973, p. 3), argues, work is not only not a "disutility" (as in neoclassical economics), and not only brings "forth the goods and services needed for a becoming existence," but also importantly it gives people the opportunity to develop their faculties and enables them to overcome their ego-centeredness "by joining with other people in a common task" (Schumacher, 1973, p. 51). Unemployment denies people these opportunities, which may be revived through JG.

Imagining the Possibilities

Proposing to combine anarchism with a government policy may seem contradictory. As Amartya Sen reminds us, however, we need to

> distinguish between (1) repressive interventions of the state in stifling liberty, initiative and enterprise, and in crippling the working of individual agency and cooperative action, and (2) the supportive role of the state in enhancing the effective freedoms of individuals (for example, in providing public education, healthcare, social safety nets, good macroeconomic policies, and in safeguarding industrial competition and epidemiological and ecological sustainability).
>
> (Sen, 2001)

The proposal here is therefore akin to what Gar Alperovitz has called "reconstruction," which he distinguishes from either reform or revolution:

> Reform is when you accept the system as it is and you try to paste up around the edges, like passing a welfare program but not touching the corporations. Revolution is when you throw the system over to change its organization. Reconstruction is changing the institutions to change the system in an evolutionary reconstructive way, not just pasting up around the edges.
>
> (Alperovitz, 1999)

The idea here is to create contexts in which counterinstitutions can be developed that promote reciprocity and mutualism. Anarchism, both "classical" and contemporary, has a rich literature filled with distinctive and provocative economic insights. There is no good reason not to consider how these might contribute to building a better economy and society. As Walden Bello has put it:

> We are talking, essentially, about an approach that consciously subordinates the logic of the market, the pursuit of cost efficiency to the values of security, equity, and social solidarity. Following Karl Polanyi, we are speaking, about re-embedding the economy in society, rather than having society driven by the economy.
>
> (Bello, 2001)

Though in mid-2012 the world economy has yet to fully recover from the "Great [i.e., Terrible] Recession," it is already on the brink of another financial crisis, the powers that be having done little or nothing to address the fundamental systemic faults, despite having applied expensive band-aids in the form of various bailouts and stimulus packages. Unemployment and underemployment, poverty, inequality, instability, and environmental degradation all are part and parcel of capitalism. Is it any wonder that economic growth does not lead to happiness (Easterlin et al., 2010)?

In this age of neoconservative globalization and economic crisis, it is necessary to envision counterhegemonic possibilities for the future. JG has been developed as a means of providing employment and income support for those who need it the most. The communitarian anarchist notion of municipal confederalism was conceived as an alternative political economic framework linking the local and regional levels of the provisioning process.

> Are these policies compatible or incompatible with the preservation of capitalism? ... Does it matter? Should we care, given the devastating costs of unemployment?
>
> (Darity, 1999, p. 496)

References

Alperovitz, Gar, 1999, "Cultures of Peace and Economic Justice," Keynote Remarks, Cultures of Peace Conference, March 5, 1999, Boston Research Center for the 21st Century, Boston, MA.

Bello, Walden, 2001, "Crisis of Legitimacy: The Revolt Against Corporate-Driven Globalization," Talk delivered on February 2, 2001, Boston Research Center for the 21st Century, Boston, MA.

Bookchin, Murray, 1993, "The Meaning of Confederalism," *Society and Nature*, Vol. 1, No. 3, pp. 41–54.

Darity, Jr., William, 1999, "Who Loses from Unemployment," *Journal of Economic Issues*, Vol. 33, No. 2, pp. 491–496.

Easterlin, Richard A. et al., 2010, "The Happiness-Income Paradox Revisited?," *Proceedings of the National Academy of Sciences*, Vol. 107, No. 52, pp. 22463–22468.

Ervin, Lorenzo Kom'Boa, 1994, *Anarchism and the Black Revolution*, Philadelphia, PA: Monkeywrench Press.

Forstater, Mathew, 2004, "Green Jobs," *International Journal of Environment, Workplace and Employment*, Vol. 1, No. 1, pp. 53–61.

Groff, Ruth, 1997, "Class Politics by Any Other Name: Organizing the Unemployed," *Studies in Political Economy*, 54, 91–117.

Hawkins, Howard, 1993, "Community Control, Workers Control, and the Cooperative Commonwealth," *Society and Nature*, Vol. 1, No. 3, pp. 55–85.

Kropotkin, Peter, 1974, *Fields, Factories, and Workshops Tomorrow*, London: Allen & Unwin.

Milani, Brian, 2000, *Designing the Green Economy*, Oxford: Rowman & Littlefield.

Rose, Nancy, 1995, *Workfare or Fair Work: Women, Welfare, and Government Work Programs*, New Brunswick, NJ: Rutgers University Press.

Roszak, Theodore, 1973, "Introduction," in E. F. Schumacher (ed.), *Small is Beautiful*, New York: Harper & Row, pp. 1–12.

Schumacher, E. F., 1973, *Small is Beautiful*, New York: Harper & Row.

Sen, Amartya, 2001, "Development as Freedom: An Approach," Lecture delivered on April 3, 2001, Boston Research Center for the 21st Century, Boston, MA.

Short, John, 1989, *The Humane City*, London: Blackwell.

Wray, L. Randall, 1998, *Understanding Modern Money*, Cheltenham, UK: Edward Elgar.

CHAPTER 7

Bring Back the WPA: Lessons from the Job Creation Programs of the 1930s

Nancy E. Rose

Recession and accompanying unemployment often brings calls to revive the WPA (Works Progress Administration), an extensive job creation program from the Great Depression of the 1930s. Although the WPA is the best known Depression era work program, it was preceded by the even more innovative and controversial FERA (Federal Emergency Relief Administration) and CWA (Civil Works Administration). Through these three programs, work was provided for 1.4–4.4 million people each month in a variety of socially useful projects at payments based on private-sector wage rates—all this at a time when the labor force was one-third of its current size. In this chapter I tell the story of these three programs, looking at the considerable accomplishments as well as the problems, especially discrimination toward women and people of color. Commonly made criticisms of "make-work" and inefficiency, which continue to characterize government job creation, are explored in terms of the "catch-22" mandates imposed on the programs—to create work for as many people as possible while avoiding both "normal government operations" and competition with the private sector.[1]

We would do well to draw inspiration and concrete ideas from these earlier programs. Further, in the context of discussions about the government as Employer of Last Resort (ELR), it is important to reclaim our history of past proposals for a permanent government job creation program. Most noteworthy from the Great Depression era were Employment Assurance, which was included in the initial draft of the Social Security Act, and the Economic Bill of Rights, proposed during the early 1940s as part of the post–World War II recovery program.

The Great Depression, the New Deal, and the Range of Job Creation Programs

The slide into the Great Depression began in August 1929 and deepened over the next three and one-half years as President Herbert Hoover resolutely clung to timeworn ideology that the government should stay out of the economy. By the time Franklin D. Roosevelt became president in March 1933, unemployment had soared to 25 percent of the entire labor force—and to 37 percent of the industrial labor force. And neither figure included "discouraged" workers who had given up looking for jobs. The continually increasing unemployment and underemployment forced down hours of work as well as wages, so that even those who still had jobs had less to spend. Other economic statistics were similarly dismal. Since the Depression began, production had fallen by one-third, prices and wages by one-quarter, and investment in new plant and equipment was at a virtual standstill. On the day Roosevelt took the office of president, 38 states had declared "bank holidays," a euphemism for shutting down, and the New York Stock Exchange and the Chicago Board of Trade had closed as well.[2]

While many of the unemployed gave in to what was seen as a "fathomless pessimism," others developed innovative forms of survival and protest.[3] Unemployed miners in western Pennsylvania dug shafts on company property in order to "bootleg" coal, an "industry" that kept the economy of that area from total collapse. Hog and dairy farmers in the Midwest formed the Farm Holiday Association, through which they organized "holidays," or strikes, to demand prices equal to the "cost of production" for their goods, and dumped milk on the highways to call attention to their concerns. Elaborate systems of barter through "self-help cooperatives" were set up, as unemployed workers traded hours of farm labor in exchange for food crops that would otherwise have rotted in the field since prices of agricultural commodities had fallen so low that it would cost more to pay workers to harvest them than would be received from their sale. Starting in early 1930, Unemployed Councils organized by the Communist Party began to lead hunger marches to demand more relief. And in a movement that resonated throughout the country, the Bonus Army of World War I veterans and their families traveled to Washington, DC, in June and July 1932 to demand early payment of their veterans' bonus. They set up a transient camp, or Hooverville, in honor of the president, to which Hoover responded by sending the cavalry, infantry, and tanks under the command of General Douglas MacArthur to set fire to the encampment.[4]

These activities led many to believe that something needed to be done to respond to the misery and protest, and to pursue other courses of action to bring about economic recovery. The policy vacuum created by the failed Hoover administration policies in conjunction with the worsening economy allowed the Roosevelt administration a great deal of room to maneuver, and the "brain trust" of mostly bright young men who Roosevelt brought to Washington, DC, developed a variety of innovative programs. Not surprisingly, policies regarding wages, employment, and relief sometimes elicited strong reactions and were changed in response to organizing by workers on the one hand and complaints by capitalists on the other.

A flurry of activity took place during the first "hundred days" of the Roosevelt presidency. The first concern was restoring a solid footing to the banking system. Upon assuming office, Roosevelt closed all of the remaining banks and Congress quickly passed the Emergency Banking Act, allowing banks to reopen only if the government assured their soundness. The reigning fiscal orthodoxy of a balanced budget was followed through with the Economy Act, which cut $500 million from federal expenditures. Further along these lines, the sizable expenditures on relief through the 1930s were labeled as emergency expenditures.

Next came legislation that established a series of agencies to address the problems in manufacturing, agriculture, and finance. The Agricultural Adjustment Act set up the Agricultural Adjustment Administration (AAA) to increase prices of agricultural commodities by reducing their supply. The National Industrial Recovery Act (NIRA) developed the National Recovery Administration (NRA), bringing together capitalists and workers under the aegis of the government to negotiate prices and wages through "codes of fair competition," and included the infamous Section 7(a) through which the federal government finally recognized the right of workers to organize unions of their own choosing.[5]

Several programs were developed to create jobs, primarily for white men. The Public Works Administration (PWA) was designed to stimulate the construction industry by contracting out projects to private-sector firms. The Tennessee Valley Authority (TVA) set up a public corporation to build dams for flood control and generate electricity. And the Civilian Conservation Corps (CCC) was established to provide work for young men in the national forests—and to get them off the roads and out of the cities where they could cause trouble.

The final issue addressed during the first 100 days of the New Deal was relief. Responding to the increasing destitution and heightened protests, the FERA was passed on May 12, 1933. In order to counteract the view that relief was shameful and to restore the "work ethic," which was assumed to be damaged by several years of inactivity, the focus was on work relief. Direct relief, that is, without requiring work, was also available at very low levels and was usually given "in kind," but the main goal was getting people back to work. The FERA was a relief program. This meant that eligibility was based on a "means test," as people had to prove that they were sufficiently needy, and payments were determined by a family's "budgetary deficiency," defined as a family's resources minus its needs.

Initially people were transferred to the FERA from existing local work programs. These had primarily been "worktests," designed to prove that people were not "lazy" and indeed deserved aid. New projects were rather quickly developed, and the rolls grew to approximately 1.7 million people, of about 12 million unemployed, by July 1933.[6]

The policies implemented through the early months of the New Deal did indeed stem the economic decline and begin a slow expansion from the abyss. Yet as the first New Deal winter approached, unemployment registered a disastrous 22 percent, and the administration believed that something grand needed to be done in order to avert another Depression winter of heightened despair and increased protest. The answer was the CWA, the most expansive jobs program thus far in US history. Established under the authority of the NIRA, as was also the case with the PWA, the CWA was intended to be an *employment* program. Payments were based on PWA wage scales and more than 2 million people were quickly added to the rolls without having to first establish eligibility for relief. Thus by January 1934 there were 4.3 million people on the CWA and another 100,000 on the Civil Works Service (CWS) program, a continuation of the FERA for women and other low-wage workers. Perhaps not surprisingly, capitalists bitterly complained that the CWA was too large, the wages paid were too high, and there was waste of government resources. In response the program was cut in January, just two months after it began, as hours were reduced and it was announced that the entire program would soon be ended.[7]

The CWA was phased out over the next two and a half months, and relief was resumed as two programs. The Rural Rehabilitation Program (RRP) was established for people in rural areas and small towns, slowly increasing to 200,000 families by April 1935.[8] Responding to the ongoing turmoil in urban areas, the primary focus was the Emergency Work Relief Program (EWRP) for the unemployed in the cities and predominantly urban areas.

The FERA lasted through spring 1935, when it was replaced by the WPA. Signed into law on April 8, 1935, the WPA was designed as a temporary measure requiring annual congressional reauthorization. WPA rolls fluctuated widely. After an initial expansion to over 3 million people by early 1936, rolls were decreased in response to ongoing criticisms and as part of the attempt to cut government spending and balance the federal budget. The reduction in government spending helped throw the economy into a sharp recession from September 1937 through May 1938, and led the Roosevelt administration to expand the work program, and more broadly, to adopt a self-consciously Keynesian model of deficit spending during recessions. A peak of 3.3 million people on the WPA was reached in November 1938, when the election of many conservatives brought the New Deal to an end and government policies in general became more restrictive. Then followed a steady decline in WPA rolls, and there were only 42,000 people left when it closed on June 30, 1943, by which time mobilization for World War II had ended the Depression and brought unemployment below 2 percent of the labor force.[9]

Eligibility and Participation on the Work Programs

The FERA and WPA were relief programs. Eligibility was based on a "means test," as applicants were investigated by the local relief agencies. The mandated process was spelled out early in the FERA to include "a prompt visit to the home; inquiry as to real property, bank accounts, and other financial resources of the family; an interview with at least one recent employer; and determination of the ability and agreement of family, relatives, friends, and churches and other organizations to assist," followed up by visits to the home at least once a month "in order to establish the continued need of those who are receiving relief." However, in practice there were wide variations in the application of these standards, depending primarily on the level of protest, availability of funds, numbers on the rolls, and local traditions and attitudes regarding relief. Relief investigations were more lenient in urban areas where organizing was greater and were more onerous in rural areas, especially in the South where the white elite fought attempts to provide aid to African Americans.[10] In addition to the "means-tested" participants, additional supervisory workers were hired through the labor market. In the WPA, this was set at no more than 10 percent of the total.[11]

Discrimination based on gender, race, class, and household status was apparent in all of the Depression era work programs. Manifested implicitly and sometimes explicitly through the criteria and selection of program participants, the primary concern of relief administrators was providing work for white male heads of households and secondarily for female and male white professional and clerical workers. As a result, throughout the 1930s white men comprised approximately three-fourth or more of all program participants.[12] To be clear, differential treatment was also apparent in the PWA, TVA, and CCC, as these programs were almost exclusively for white males.

Differential treatment by gender and race in all of these New Deal programs reflected societal sexism and racism. Women encountered difficulties establishing eligibility for the work programs since they were assumed to belong in the home taking care of their families, regardless of the reality of their circumstances. Regulations stipulated that only heads of household could be given work, and if a man was present he was assumed to be the household head. As explained by Donald S. Howard, whose tome on the WPA remains the most comprehensive, relief administrators wanted to "put some brake upon women's eagerness to be the family breadwinner, wage recipient, and controller of the family pocketbook." Wanting to "protect the WPA program against possible public criticisms for employing 'too many women,'" they were kept to less than one-sixth of the rolls even though they comprised one-quarter of the labor force.[13] Further, as described in the *Final Report on the WPA Program,* concern about male heads of household eventually led to selecting the husband of the house instead of a younger and stronger male because that would "weaken the responsibility and authority of the family head and injure the family structure."[14]

People of color, both women and men, faced the most severe hurdles in establishing eligibility and, in general, obtaining fair treatment on the work programs. While some Mexican Americans were on the work rolls in the Southeast, most of the people of color who managed to get placements were African Americans.[15] A common means of discrimination was using different standards of need based on race. As unapologetically explained by historian Donald S. Howard: "Negro workers, accustomed to relatively low standards of living, may be denied WPA employment on the grounds that they are not in need whereas workers accustomed to relatively higher standards of living may be declared eligible for such employment even though they have as large and possibly larger resources than the former."[16] When they were certified as eligible for the work programs, people of color received lower payments, and were usually placed in segregated projects—that is, if they could find placements at all.

Differences according to class were evident throughout the work programs, as professional and clerical workers were accorded special treatment. This included more easily establishing eligibility, receiving higher payments, and being placed in special "white-collar" projects. While this preferential treatment extended to all whites, both women and men, the same did not hold true for people of color. Instead, for both white-collar and skilled workers, if people of color managed to be certified as eligible, they were usually placed in unskilled positions. Some of these examples are telling. For example, the many surveys conducted through the programs were usually staffed by whites. Alfred Edgar Smith, WPA assistant administrator and Labor Relations staff advisor, who wrote reports about the status of African Americans in the WPA, succinctly explained that "whites do not like to be interviewed by Negroes." These practices extended to the relief agencies themselves, as few African Americans were employed as caseworkers or administrators.[17] Progress was made in the WPA Federal Arts Project, as many blacks were involved in these activities, including integrated theater productions. This roused the ire of conservatives, who complained that "there is no distinction in the cast. The colored and white are mixed together, dance together, and the actors are the same."[18] They were also angered by the content of some of the productions, particularly the *Living Newspaper,* which combined newsreel clips, radio shows, and acting to present contemporary issues from a progressive perspective. As a result, as part of the 1939 restrictions Congress prohibited the use of federal funds for the entire Federal Arts Project.[19]

Struggles over Work Program Payment Policies

While policies regarding eligibility provoked little criticism throughout the 1930s, the same was not true of rules regarding determination of payments, especially during the FERA and the CWA. Employers argued that rates were too high, consequently attracting workers to the programs instead of private-sector jobs. Most persistent in their complaints were Southerners, who worried that any alternatives to low-wage work threatened the supply of African Americans in agriculture and domestic service. Workers responded that low rates on the work programs would further depress private-sector wage rates. Organized labor, which increased in numbers and strength through the 1930s, was especially insistent about the need to set work relief rates at the levels of prevailing market rates. Relief administrators tried to balance these positions, changing policies sometimes dramatically during the first two years of the programs. Yet they were more inclined toward setting relief rates at higher levels in order to boost low private sector wages and to thereby "increase the purchasing power of the masses," as this would quickly lead to increased spending and thereby contribute to economic recovery.

When the FERA began, total payments were determined by "budgetary deficiency," which was divided by the relevant work relief wage rate to arrive at the hours of work. (For example, if a family's budgetary deficiency was $80/month and the prevailing wage rate was 50 cents/hour, the family member on the rolls could work 120 hours/month.) At first, this was based solely on prevailing market rates for similar work. However, wanting to raise wage rates as low as 10 cents/hour in the South, in July 1933 the relief administration set a minimum work relief rate of 30 cents/hour. Not surprisingly, this policy drew unremitting criticism from the business sector in general, and from Southerners in particular, until it was rescinded in November 1934.[20]

Complaints from capitalists intensified during the CWA. Since the CWA was an employment program, budgetary deficiency was abandoned and the higher pay scale used on the PWA was adopted. Participants worked 30 hours/week at pay rates determined by their level of skill and area of the country, with the PWA minimum of 40 cents/hour. Yet the CWA was primarily for white males, as the old 30 cents/hour minimum was retained in road projects, which provided work for unskilled blue-collar workers, some of whom were African American, and through the CWS program, which continued FERA projects primarily for women.[21]

When the FERA resumed in spring 1934, budgetary deficiency was again used to determine payments, with the pre–CWA 30 cents/hour minimum rate. Yet even this was deemed insufficient by the business sector, and following the Democrats' resounding victory in the November 1934 elections, the contentious 30 cents/hour minimum rate was abandoned entirely. Prevailing rates were adopted, resulting in work relief rates between 10 and 20 cents/hour through much of the South by the following January. Seeming to anticipate these results, relief officials in some southern states appealed to local agencies to prevent work relief wage rates from falling below $.10 per hour.[22]

Wage rate policies provoked far less controversy on the WPA. Wanting to approximate prevailing wage rates for similar work, total monthly payments were based on a scale using three factors: region of the country, degree of urbanization, and skill level. Initially this was based on a "security wage," whereby all participants worked between 120 and 140 hours per month. In 1936, under pressure from organized labor, the prevailing wage policy was resumed, and lasted until the restrictions that began in 1939 when all WPA participants worked 130 hours per month.[23]

In spite of the basically progressive bent of work relief wage rate policies, some regulations contributing to the maintenance of private-sector wages rate remained in place in all three work programs. Most importantly, program workers were always required to accept private-sector employment if it was offered, and pay differentials based on gender, race, and class were transferred to the work programs.[24]

The requirement to take private-sector employment led to instances of removing workers from the rolls when they were needed elsewhere. This was an important issue throughout the South, especially for people of color, as large supplies of available workers effectively maintained extremely low rates in agriculture and domestic service. Thad Holt, Director of the Alabama Relief Administration, described one such illustrative situation in Alabama in September 1934, explaining that at least 9,000 day laborers had been dropped from the relief rolls, many of whom would not be able to find work, and that consequently "anybody applying for cotton-pickers can have ten of them for the job."[25] Federal relief officials condoned this practice, and issued a directive stating that "(the FERA) not only approves this procedure, but insists upon its being followed by those States in which conditions of seasonal employment warrant such action." Further trying to ensure that it would be followed, relief administrators cut federal aid to states in which cotton and tobacco were grown.[26]

This policy continued in the WPA, disproportionately affecting black women. In January 1937, for example, the *Birmingham News* reported that 150 African American women were dropped from the WPA rolls "because of sharply increased demand for servants." And a North Carolina relief official described their actions:

> In April, 1936, all sewing rooms, both white and colored, in the strawberry section of this county were closed because of the fact that labor was

> available to these women both in picking and packing of strawberries. Since employment was available in the tobacco fields, these rooms were not re-opened until after the tobacco season, which was sometime during the month of November, 1936.[27]

Maintaining race- and gender-based wage differentials sometimes led to adopting different pay scales. For example, in Houston, Texas, white teachers earned $1.00 per hour, while black teachers earned only $.60.[28] And the situation in Jackson, Mississippi, was described by Evangelist John R. Perkins:

> We received our work cards marked 40 cents per hour
> And went to work without any regret
> On Saturday two hundred colored men was deceived
> And 30 cents was all we could get . . .
> We only want Uncle Sam to know
> They did not treat us right
> They cut our wages to 30 cents per hour
> Yet 40 cents was paid to the white.[29]

This was not unique to the work programs, as disparities were incorporated into the NRA "codes of fair competition" that set industry wages. Gender wage scales were somewhat apologetically explained by an NRA official: "Numerous differentials of various kinds can be found in the codes which it may be difficult to defend on purely logical grounds, but they represent long established customs."[30] More generally in the relief programs, the classification of people of color as unskilled regardless of their skill level or professional status relegated them to the lowest paid work.

Innovation and Controversy over the Content of the Projects

The range of projects developed through these work programs continues to serve as a source of inspiration for possibilities of what can be accomplished in job creation programs. Construction projects provided work for blue-collar men.[31] An assortment of "white-collar projects" were developed for professional and clerical workers hard hit by unemployment, some of which remain examples of expansive federal support for the arts. And several types of "production-for-use" projects were set up for blue-collar women and men.

The projects developed in the FERA, CWA, and WPA were often lightning rods for criticisms of the programs. Most importantly, they were mandated to create the maximum amount of work with the allocated funds, while avoiding competition with private-sector industry or replacing normal government operations. While this was logical, it left the projects open to charges that they were unnecessary "make-work" and inefficient, a notion captured during this era by the term, "boondoggle."

The main type of project in all three programs was construction, which absorbed approximately three-fourths of the funds throughout the 1930s. The results are indeed impressive and include construction and repair of the following: more than 1 million miles of roads; approximately 200,000 buildings (e.g., schools, libraries, courthouses, firehouses, armories); tens of thousands of recreational facilities (e.g., parks, stadiums, swimming and wading pools); several thousand public utility plants; miles of sewers, drainage ditches, and electric power lines; thousands of flood and erosion control projects (e.g., firebreaks, retaining walls, levees); and several hundred airports. In order to create as much work as possible with the allocated funds, these projects were required to use a maximum amount of labor and a minimum amount of machinery. Indeed, road construction was often called "pick and shovel" projects as workers typically used these simple tools instead of grading and paving machines. While this put more people to work, it meant that the projects were clearly inefficient compared to the more capital-intensive industry standards.[32]

The second major category of work was "white-collar projects," developed to make use of the skills of professional and clerical workers and to provide a variety of services. These served as an important source of work for white women and men, although people of color were underrepresented.[33] Even though they were routinely criticized as "boondoggles," white-collar projects became an accepted component of the Depression era work programs. They included conducting surveys assessing the need for relief among various groups in the population (e.g., transients, rural families, youths); research on a variety of economic and social topics (e.g., housing facilities, health surveys, studies of the effects of automation); public records projects (e.g., indexing deeds and mortgages, mapping, and codifying municipal ordinances); historical records surveys (preserving records of historical importance); research assistance in universities; and gathering oral histories of former slaves (which have become an invaluable resource for historians).

The other major white-collar component of the program, termed "public activities," was similarly broad. It included education projects for children in rural areas and for adults in urban areas (primarily adult general education, as well as literacy, vocational education, parent education, and worker education); supervising recreation programs; and working in libraries and museums. It also included the WPA Federal Arts project, which remains an inspiring example of extensive federal support for the arts. Artists created paintings, sculptures, murals, posters, and handicrafts, which were then displayed in public institutions. Writers produced a series of guidebooks about each state. Musicians, actors, and stage personnel formed WPA symphony orchestras, bands, and theater troupes that gave performances around the country.[34] Other service projects came under the heading of "welfare activities": housekeeping aide projects provided work for blue-collar women and assistance for relief families through home visits in times of illness or other emergencies; and public health projects were a source of work for skilled health professionals on relief (doctors, dentists, nurses, pharmacists) as well as for nonprofessional "helpers" in hospitals, clinics, and schools.[35]

The third category was projects in which consumer goods were produced. Commonly known as "production-for-use" or "production-for-use and distribution," they had a turbulent history.[36] None of the goods were sold through normal market channels, but were given only to relief recipients, who had minimal resources after several years of the depression, or used in other relief projects or public institutions (e.g., hospitals). Yet some of the projects came under fire for competing unfairly with private enterprise; as a result, they were quickly curtailed or ended entirely.

The initial production-for-use projects were expanded from work relief predating the New Deal. These were accepted forms of work relief, which provided an important source of "in kind" direct relief for others on the rolls, and therefore elicited relatively little criticism. Most common were "labor-intensive workrooms" in which women sewed and mended garments, bedding (e.g. sheets and comforters), and other items such as rag rugs and corn brooms. While most of the work was initially done by hand, the sewing rooms became increasingly mechanized throughout the 1930s, as cutting rooms were often centralized and foot treadle and electric machines replaced some of the hand sewing. Subsistence gardens were common throughout the Depression era. Expanded from their limited use before the FERA to encompass both community gardens and home gardens, they were complemented by projects in which the produce was preserved. Also continued from pre-FERA work relief was fuel procurement, primarily chopping wood. And a new project was developed in which aid was provided to the self-help cooperatives that had been set up earlier in the depression, since the AAA's program had increased prices of agricultural commodities and made farmers unwilling to continue the previous barter arrangements.[37]

Responding to criticisms of the early FERA and CWA for creating unnecessary "make-work," production-for-use tripled in the five months after the CWA ended as clearly useful goods were produced in innovative and often controversial projects.[38] Aid to self-help cooperatives was further expanded as participants engaged in a broad range of activities in addition to farm labor, such as carpentry and house repair, repairing shoes and appliances, and operating commissaries, cafeterias, barber shops, and beauty salons. A mattress-making project extended the work in labor-intensive sewing rooms, as women sewed mattresses and comforters by hand on frames built by men on relief, using some of the surplus cotton that had been taken off the market by the AAA. The projects for canning garden produce were expanded into centers to slaughter and preserve animals dying from the severe drought, and to produce and repair goods, primarily shoes and wearing apparel, from the hides, pelts, and wool. The most controversial of all the new projects were those in which relief recipients were put to work in factories that had been partially or entirely shut down and rented from their owners by state or local relief administrations. Commonly known as the Ohio Plan since it was most extensive in that state, relief workers produced clothing (e.g., long underwear, coats, knitted goods), furniture (primarily wooden beds and kitchen-type chairs), metal ware (stoves, heaters, and skillets), china, and blankets. Additional factories for production of clothing (long underwear and knitted goods) were also leased in Michigan and in Maine, and two knitting mills were reopened in Massachusetts. Yet the Ohio Plan most vividly revealed the contradictions of production-for-profit, as the government put idle workers in idle factories to produce useful consumer goods since capitalists were failing to do so.[39]

The new production-for-use projects quickly came under fire. In August 1934, the American Liberty League was formed to provide a more direct voice for industrial giants such as DuPont and General Motors, as well as the Chamber of Commerce and the National Association of Manufacturers, and quickly focused some of their indignation on production-for-use and more generally what they saw as a developing welfare state that was encroaching on their territory. The League's views were clearly articulated by the Joint Business Conference for Economic

Recovery, held in December 1934. In the *Conference Report*, which was entered into the *Congressional Digest,* they complained that projects were inefficient and competed unfairly with the private sector, and that the government was forcing up private-sector wage rates by paying relief workers too much, which created labor shortages, especially of low-wage labor. According to the League, relief projects were impeding the return of business confidence, increasing unemployment, and undermining the recovery. Instead of the offending work programs, they argued that direct relief should replace work relief whenever possible, only construction projects should be used, people should be paid no more than they would receive for direct relief, and all relief should be reduced in order to balance the federal budget. Propounding time-worn conservative philosophy, they claimed that

> the most effective solution of the problem of unemployment and relief is the creation of such confidence between industry and the government that business can proceed with plans to develop new industries, to enlarge existing enterprises, and freely to place private capital in the investment field.[40]

And they indignantly declared that "(g)overnment competition with private business leads toward socialism." *Business Week* clarified their concerns, explaining that the business sector was not really worried about competition from the existing small scale of production-for-use, but was concerned instead about "the uncomfortable thought that government manufacture might be expanded widely and might become permanent."[41] Business-sector criticisms were considered too strong to ignore, and throughout the fall of 1934 the scope of the work programs was considerably narrowed.

Throughout the rest of the 1930s most of the production-for-use was carried out in the sewing rooms. These absorbed a full 93.5 percent of consumer goods production in the WPA, as 383 million garments and 118 other articles were produced. In spite of the earlier fight against it, mattress-making was brought back briefly in 1939 and 1940, this time as part of the sewing rooms for women instead of as a separate project. However, capitalist objections again led to their demise. Most of the remaining production-for-use activities in the WPA involved gardening and canning, which were extended to food preparation and distribution. Particularly important was the school lunch program, as over 1.2 billion meals were served using surplus agricultural commodities and food grown in relief gardens.[42]

Employment Assurance, the Economic Bill of Rights, and the 1945 Full Employment Bill

The Great Depression era saw the development of two proposals that would have established a permanent federal jobs program, and essentially committed the government to functioning as the ELR. It is helpful to review these in order to remember that the idea of ELR is not new, but indeed has a history in the United States.

Employment Assurance would have established a work program as part of the Social Security Act, which continues to provide the basis for welfare and social insurance programs in the United States. It promised public employment after a person's unemployment compensation was exhausted, as well as to "able-bodied workers" not covered by unemployment compensation, and its rationale was spelled out in the final report of the Committee on Economic Security, which drafted the legislation:

> While it will not always be necessary to have public-employment projects to give employment assurance, it should be recognized as a permanent policy of the Government and not merely as an emergency measure.[43]

Although it was included in the initial draft of the Social Security Act, called the Economic Security Act to reflect its broader scope, it was eliminated in subsequent committee deliberations.

Support for including a work program as part of a permanent federal relief system came from progressives and high-level relief administrators, as well as from more mainstream groups, most importantly the International City Managers' Association and the US Conference of Mayors. Implicit in their backing was the understanding that Employment Assurance would focus on white men and would be clearly separate from direct relief.[44] And Harry Hopkins, chief of all three work programs, added his recommendation, proposing a Federal Work Relief Corporation that would implement Employment Assurance as a separate work program that he described as a "sort of permanent CWA."[45]

The battles over the FERA and CWA took their toll on the plans for Employment Assurance. Conservatives in the Roosevelt administration, who tended to reflect views of capitalists, argued strenuously against the implementation of any type of permanent work program. In particular, administration financial advisors "threw their weight against a form of action that might have seemed to associate work relief efforts with the enactment of the beginnings of a permanent structure of security," since they "preferred to advance the works program as a strictly temporary expedient."[46] Thus, instead of including a work program either as part of the Social Security Act itself or as a separate permanent program, public employment was continued in the temporary WPA, intended to meet the emergency needs of the Depression and to end when it was no longer needed.

Support for the government as ELR arose again in the early 1940s during the process of planning for the post–World War II era. The National Resources Planning Board (NRPB) had been established by Roosevelt in 1933 to help plan for and coordinate public works, and thereby help prevent long-term secular stagnation. The culmination of the NRPB's work came in reports published in 1942 and 1943 planning for the postwar economy. In these reports, the NRPB returned to the idea of Employment Assurance as proposed in the initial draft of the Social Security Act. Insisting that "our economy must provide work for all who are able and willing to work," the 1943 *Report* proposed a "New Bill of Rights" that would extend the political bill of rights in the US constitution to enumerated rights for economic security. This would include "(t)he right to work, usefully and creatively through the productive years" and would involve the "(f)ormal *acceptance by the Federal Government of responsibility* (emphasis theirs) for insuring jobs at decent pay to all those able to work regardless of whether or not they can pass a means test," carried out through a permanent "Work Administration" that would create "all kinds of *socially useful work* (emphasis theirs) other than construction."[47]

Although the NRPB was terminated in 1943, the idea of an "economic bill of rights" was advocated by President Roosevelt in his 1944 State of the Union address. Asserting that "true individual freedom cannot exist without economic security and independence," his recommendations included the "right to a useful and remunerative job" as well as the "right to earn enough to provide adequate food and clothing, and recreation."[48]

The commitment to national planning and government as ELR was incorporated into the original draft of the Full Employment bill of 1945. Affirming that "all Americans able to work and seeking work have the right to useful, remunerative, regular, and full-time employment," it would have obligated the federal government to pursue policies designed to ensure full employment. This would be carried out through an annual "National Production and Employment Budget," which would estimate the amount of (both public and private) expected investment and the level of spending needed for full employment and commit the federal government to fill this investment gap, if necessary with deficit spending. While the Full Employment Bill did not explicitly contain a public employment program, an opening existed through establishment of an agency similar to the NRPB.[49]

But the results were minimal, as the Full Employment Bill of 1945 became the watered-down Employment Act of 1946. An unequivocal commitment to "full employment" was replaced with tempered support for "maximum employment"; in the context of the debates, this was clearly understood as less than "full employment." Instead of the "National Production and Employment Budget" and its planning mechanism there was only an advisory body, the Council of Economic Advisors, and an annual report to the president. And in place of the obligation to use federal deficit spending to increase demand and create jobs, there remained only a vague statement that the government would create favorable economic "conditions." As Ohio Senator Robert Taft explained to fellow Republicans, "I do not think any Republican need fear voting for the bill because of any apprehension that there is a victory in the passage of the full employment bill, because there is no full employment bill anymore."[50]

Lessons for Today: Responses to Criticisms of Government Job Creation Programs

In making the case for the government as ELR, it is helpful to draw lessons from the Depression era programs. In doing so, it is particularly important to develop responses to time-worn criticisms that inevitably arise whenever public employment programs are mentioned. Indeed, the much smaller Public Employment Program (PEP) and Public Service Employment (PSE) set up through the Comprehensive Employment and Training Act (CETA) during the 1970s were targets of many of the same criticisms faced by the programs in the 1930s.

The most common charges made toward the Depression era work programs were that they were too costly, local administrations were prone to graft and corruption, participants were paid too much, the work was unnecessary and inefficient "make-work," and some of the projects competed unfairly with private enterprise. The first two complaints—of graft and corruption, and excessive expenditures—are often made, sometimes justifiably, about government programs. The most telling objections are the last three since they have to do with the contradictory nature of the programs as simultaneously work and relief, and with the "logic of the market," that is, the profitable production of goods and services in the private sector.

The work programs were periodically criticized for providing payments that were too high, which attracted potential workers from private-sector jobs, complaints that were especially intense during the CWA. These charges continued even though less than one-third of the millions of people who remained unemployed throughout the 1930s were on the work programs at any time (and less than two-fifths at the height of the CWA), thereby assuring employers of a more than ample supply of labor. Further, large supplies of workers were assured by the mandate to accept private-sector jobs if they became available, and by the practice of removing groups of people from the rolls when there was any chance of a potential shortage of workers, especially in agriculture and domestic service. The real issue seems to have been the very existence of public employment as an alternative to private-sector jobs, especially for low-wage workers in the South.

Throughout the 1930s, the programs were plagued by accusations that the projects were inefficient and unnecessary "make-work"—or "boondoggles." Indeed, these criticisms had some validity. Yet they followed inevitably from regulations to put as many people as possible to work with the allocated funds and to avoid replacing normal government operations. Thus although some of the projects became increasingly mechanized as the 1930s wore on, more often they were characterized by a maximum amount of labor and a minimum amount of machinery, as widely seen in the "pick and shovel" construction projects. This created work for more people—but was inefficient compared to the more capital-intensive production methods commonly used in the private sector. Nels Anderson, Director of Labor Relations in the WPA, clarified an ongoing result of the catch-22 situation inherent in the contradictory mandates: "If a project is useful it is sure to be criticized because it is competitive, while if it is non-competitive it is just as likely to be condemned by the same critics as not being useful."[51] Additionally, the charge that much of the work was unnecessary was bolstered by requirements to avoid replacing normal government operations. This made sense, since the government should continue to provide services, hiring workers through the labor market to do so—but virtually by definition it left the programs open to the perception that the work was not really necessary.

Criteria of efficiency warrants further exploration. Government programs are often seen as inefficient simply because they are not based on profits, an ideological view assuming that the very lack of a profit motive automatically renders the government inefficient when compared with the private sector. Since the early 1980s it has led to government at various levels contracting out services from garbage collection to prisons to be run by private-sector firms. And as we have seen repeatedly, criteria of efficiency and profitably often have disastrous effects for working people, as jobs are eliminated in the interests of increasing profits for owners.

Most instructive during the Great Depression were allegations of unfair competition since those most clearly reveal the inability of an economic system based on production-for-profit to meet people's needs. New and innovative production-for-use projects were condemned even though years of depression had left people with so little money that, although the composition of what they bought might have changed, their total purchases were not curtailed by receiving goods made on relief projects. As J.C. Lindsey, a regional engineer for the FERA, explained in response to accusations that FERA shoe repair shops would take business away from private merchants: "If these shoes were not repaired or furnished by us, the men and women for whom we are doing this work would simply be without shoes."[52]

Some federal relief officials in the 1930s responded to these criticisms by challenging their appropriateness for judging the work programs. Harry Hopkins questioned the criteria normally used:

> In the relief business where our raw material is misery and our finished product nothing more than amelioration, effectiveness has to be measured in less ambitious terms than success. That word applies better to marginal profit, cash or otherwise. Relief deals with human insolvency.[53]

And Nels Anderson, Director of Labor Relations in the WPA, succinctly asserted that the government differed from private industry as it was "guided by social rather than profit motivations."[54]

Following this line of reasoning, we could argue that the criteria used to evaluate job creation programs needs to be challenged, and measures based on the logic of production-for-profit should be replaced by more fitting assessments grounded in people's needs. The FERA, CWA, and WPA provide inspiration and concrete models for programs in the current era. They demonstrate that the federal government does indeed have the capacity to create jobs for millions of people. And the projects undertaken in the 1930s could be replicated today. Throughout the country, repairing our crumbling infrastructure could provide work for millions of people. A variety of projects could be developed to provide services. And it makes sense to again put the unemployed back to work in factories that have been shut down as their operations have been moved overseas. Differential treatment by gender and race, which were so common in the 1930s programs, could be corrected in the present. It is time to bring back the extensive and innovative job creation programs of the 1930s, this time as a permanent program and in ways that fundamentally address the needs of women and people of color as well as white men.

Notes

1. In 1939, the name was changed to Work Projects Administration. For a more in-depth history of these programs, see Nancy E. Rose, *Put to Work: The WPA and Public Employment in the Great Depression* (New York: Monthly Review Press, 1994; 2nd ed. 2009).
2. US Bureau of the Census, *Historical Statistics of the United States, Colonial Times to 1970* (Washington, DC: Government Printing Office, 1975), p. 126; and Lester V. Chandler, *America's Greatest Depression, 1929–1941* (New York: Harper and Row, 1970), pp. 4, 7, 21, 23.
3. This "fathomless pessimism" was described in Louis Adamic, *My America, 1928–1938* (London: Hamish Hamilton, 1939), p. 309.
4. Lively accounts of these activities can be found in ibid.; William E. Leuchtenburg, *Franklin D. Roosevelt and the New Deal, 1932–1940* (New York: Harper Colyphon, 1963); Irving Bernstein, *The Lean Years: A History of the American Worker, 1920–1933* (Baltimore: Penguin Books, 1960); and David A. Shannon, *The Great Depression* (Englewood Cliffs, NJ: Prentice-Hall, 1960).
5. Additional New Deal legislation addressing the crisis in finance included the Securities and Exchange Commission, the Federal Deposit Insurance Corporation, the Glass-Steagall Act separating commercial and investment banking, and expansion of the Federal Reserve System.
6. Works Projects Administration, *Final Statistical Report of the Federal Emergency Relief Administration* (Washington, DC: US Government Printing Office, 1942), p. 46.
7. Doris Carothers, WPA Research Monograph VI, *Chronology of the Federal Emergency Relief Administration, May 12, 1933 to December 31, 1935* (Washington, DC: Government Printing Office, 1937; New York: Da Capo Press, 1971), p. 41.
8. "Rural Rehabilitation Program-1," in Carothers, *Chronology of the Federal Emergency Relief Administration,* pp. 51, 57; "The Rural Rehabilitation Program," *Monthly Report of the Federal Emergency Relief Administration* (August 1935), pp. 14–20.
9. Federal Works Agency, *Final Report on the WPA Program, 1935–1943* (Washington, DC: Government Printing Office, 1947; reprint edition, Westport, CT: Greenwood Press, 1976), p. 28.

10. *Monthly Report of the Federal Emergency Relief Administration* (May 22–June 30, 1933), pp. 11–12; Josephine Chapin Brown, *Public Relief 1929–1939* (New York: Holt, Rinehart and Winston, 1940; reprint edition New York: Octagon Books, 1971), pp. 231–237.
11. "Emergency Work Program," *Monthly Report of the Federal Emergency Relief Administration* (March 1934), p. 5; Arthur E. Burns, "Federal Emergency Relief Administration," in *The Municipal Yearbook 1937,* p. 396; Donald. S. Howard, *The WPA and Federal Relief Policy* (1943; New York: Da Capo Press, 1973), pp. 359–372.
12. Federal Works Agency, *Final Report on the WPA Program,* p. 45.
13. Howard, *The WPA*, p. 279.
14. Federal Works Agency, *Final Report on the WPA Program,* p. 17.
15. Mexican Americans in the southwest were periodically treated as "aliens." As the Depression continued, approximately 400,000 Mexican Americans, many of whom were US citizens, were deported to Mexico, and in April 1936, Colorado Governor Johnson declared martial law on the southern border (with New Mexico) and called out the National Guard to prevent Mexicans and Mexican Americans from entering the state. Sarah Deutsch, *No Separate Refuge: Culture, Class, and Gender on an Anglo-Hispanic Frontier in the American Southwest, 1880–1940* (New York: Oxford University Press, 1987), p. 165.
16. Howard, *The WPA*, p. 291.
17. Alfred Edgar Smith, *Highlights of Activities* (September 1938), p. 3, in National Archives, Record Group 69, WPA Series 11: no. 102: Public Relations. In February 1935 a decimal classification system was adopted for FERA, CWA, and WPA records in the National Archives. Documents obtained before this time were included in the CWA Series #2 and the FERA Old General Subject Series #8 (FERA Series 8), while documents gathered after this date were filed in FERA New General Subject Series #9 (FERA Series 9) and series for each state (FERA Series 10). The decimal classification system was continued in the WPA in the General Subject Series #11 (WPA Series 11) and in the State Series #12 (WPA Series 12).
18. Cited in Howard, *The WPA,* pp. 294–295.
19. Ibid., pp. 138–139, 294–295; and Federal Works Agency, *Final Report on the WPA Program*, p. 63.
20. Doris Carothers, WPA Research Monograph VI, *Chronology of the Federal Emergency Relief Administration, May 12, 1933 to December 31, 1935* (Washington, DC: Government Printing Office, 1937; New York: Da Capo Press, 1971), pp. 9, 12; and Arthur E. Burns, "Work Relief Wage Policies, 1930–1936," *Monthly Report of the Federal Emergency Relief Administration* (June 1936), p. 32.
21. Carothers, *Chronology of the Federal Emergency Relief Administration*, pp. 28–30, 33.

22. Burns, "Work Relief Wage Policies," p. 37; Carothers, *Chronology of the Federal Emergency Relief Administration*, p. 45; and "Survey of Common Labor Rates Paid on the Work Program," *Monthly Report of the Federal Emergency Relief Administration* (January 1935), pp. 5, 7.
23. FWA, *Final Report on the WPA,* pp. 21–27; Howard, *The WPA,* pp. 214–216; and Arthur W. Macmahon, John D. Millett, and Gladys Ogden, *The Administration of Federal Work Relief* (New York: Da Capo Press, 1971), pp. 157–161.
24. Federal Works Agency, *Final Report on the WPA Program*, pp. 23–25; Macmahon et al., *The Administration of Federal Work Relief,* pp. 151–157; and Howard, *The WPA*, Chapter 6.
25. Letter from Thad Holt to Harry Hopkins, Sept. 21, 1934, in National Archives, Record Group 69, FERA Series #8, Cotton Reports.
26. "Removal from Relief Rolls to Meet Labor Shortages," *Monthly Report of the Federal Emergency Relief Administration* (July 1935), p. 49.
27. Alfred Edgar Smith, *Negro Project Workers: An Annual Report of Matters Incident to the Administration of Race Relations in Federal Unemployment Relief for the Year 1936* (January 1937), p. 3, in National Archives, Record Group 69, WPA Series 11; Alfred Edgar Smith, *Highlights of Activities* (Jan. 16, 1937), p. 1-A; and Alfred Edgar Smith, *Highlights of Activities* (May, 1937), p. 6.
28. Smith, *Negro Project Workers*, pp. 4–7; Alfred E. Smith, "The Negro and Relief," *Monthly Report of the Federal Emergency Relief Administration* (March 1936), p. 14; National Archives, Record Group 69, CWA Series #2, Interracial Correspondence; and Howard, *The WPA*, p. 292.
29. Ibid.
30. Mary Elizabeth Pidgeon, US Women's Bureau Bulletin No. 155, *Women in the Economy of the United States of America: A Summary Report* (Washington, DC: US Government Printing Office, 1937; Da Capo Press, 1975), pp. 9–25.
31. Some women were given work conducting surveys on construction projects.
32. Federal Works Agency, *Final Statistical Report of the Federal Emergency Relief Administration*, pp. 54, 57; Federal Works Agency, *Final Report on the WPA Program*, pp. 122, 131–132; and Corrington Gill, "The Civil Works Administration," in Clarence E. Ridley and Orin F. Nolting, eds., *The Municipal Yearbook 1937: The Authoritative Resume of Activities and Statistical Data of American Cities* (Chicago: The International City Managers' Association, 1937), pp. 57, 424–425.
33. From one-third to one-half of those on the projects throughout the 1930s were women, and approximately one-third of all women on the programs were involved in white-collar work. A FERA survey found that people of color comprised only 5 percent of the white-collar project rolls, a figure that was probably slightly higher in the WPA. "Relief for White-Collar Workers," *Monthly Report of the Federal Emergency Relief Administration*

(December 1935), pp. 59–64; Federal Works Agency, *Final Report on the WPA Program*, pp. 44, 59–67; and "Emergency Work Program," *Monthly Report of the Federal Emergency Relief Administration* (May 1934), pp. 11–12.

34. Federal Works Agency, *Final Report on the WPA Program*, pp. 60–67, 122.
35. Ibid., pp. 44, 68–70,133; and National Archives, Record Group 69, WPA Series 11, #212.2: Welfare Projects, and #230: Women's Work.
36. For a more extensive discussion of these projects, see Nancy E. Rose, "Production-for-Use or Production-for-Profit?: Contradictions of Consumer Goods Production in 1930s Work Relief," *Review of Radical Political Economics*, Vol. 20, No. 1 (Spring 1988): 46–61.
37. P. A. Kerr, "Production-for-Use and Distribution in Work Relief Activities," *Monthly Report of the Federal Emergency Relief Administration* (Sept. 1935); Trend of Developments in the Sewing and Mattress Program, pp. 2–3, in National Archives, Record Group 69, WPA Series 11, #218.1: Sewing and Mattress Projects, 1940; Division of Self-Help Cooperatives, Federal Emergency Relief Administration, *Self-Help Cooperatives: An Introductory Study* (Washington, DC: Government Printing Office, 1934); Clark Kerr and Paul S. Taylor, "The Self-Help Cooperatives in California," in *Essays in Social Economics in Honor of Jessica Blanche Peixotto* (1935; Freeport, NY: Books for Libraries Press, Inc., 1967); and Federal Works Agency, *Final Report on the WPA Program*, p. 44.
38. While production-for-use provided work for only 5.4 percent of relief workers in May 1934, they grew to over 15 percent of the rolls by the following October. Kerr, "Production-for-Use and Distribution in Work Relief Activities," pp. 2, 5.
39. Kerr, "Production-for-Use," p. 12; State Relief Commission of Ohio, *The State Relief Commission of Ohio and Its Activities, April 1932 to January 1, 1935* (Columbus, OH: Carroll Press, 1935), p. 53; Joanna C. Colcord, "Ohio Produces for Ohioans," *The Survey* 70,12 (1934): 371–373; Raymond G. Swing, "EPIC and the Ohio Plan," *The Nation* (October 3, 1934): 379–381; and "Operation of Idle Factories," *Monthly Labor Review* (December 1934): 1311–1319.
40. *Congressional Digest* (January 1935), pp. 27–29.
41. Letter from J.C. Lindsey to Perry A. Fellows, Administrative Office, FERA, 10 December 1934, in National Archives, FERA Series 8: Goods, Production of, for Unemployed. Two full boxes of letters under the heading "Production-for-Use Complaints," can be found in the National Archives. National Archives, Record Group 69, Series 8, Boxes #16 and #17. See also, *Congressional Digest* (January 1935), pp. 27–29; and FERA Factories," *Business Week*, 28 July 1934, p. 22.
42. Federal Works Agency, *Final Report on the WPA Program*, pp. 68, 122, and 133; and Bureau of Agricultural Economics, *The School Lunch Program and*

Agricultural Surplus Disposal (October 1941), in National Archives, WPA Series 11, #212.2: School Lunch Program.

43. US, Congress, House, *Hearings before the Committee on Ways and Means, 21 January–12 February 1935, on H.R. 4120, The Economic Security Act,* 74th Cong., 1st sess., p. 25.
44. "Permanent Relief Asked by Mayors from Roosevelt," *The New York Times,* 23 September 1934, p. 1; "The Mayors Confer with the President," *The American City* (October 1934), p. 39; and "Mayors Demand Vast New Works," *The New York Times,* 25 November 1934, p. 2.
45. "Hopkins Envisions New Era in Relief," *The New York Times,* 24 August 1934, p. 17; and "Flurry Over Hopkins Finds His <EPIA> at Work," *The New York Times, 2* December 1934, Sect. IV, p. 1. "EPIA" was a play on the End Poverty in California (EPIC) program that had been proposed by Upton Sinclair during his campaign for governor of California.
46. Macmahon et al., *The Administration of Federal Work Relief,* p. 27.
47. National Resources Planning Board, *National Resources Development Report for 1943, Part I. Post-War Plan and Program* (Washington, DC: US Government Printing Office, January 1943), p. 17. For discussions of the National Resources Planning Board, see, for example, Marion Clawson, *New Deal Planning: The National Resources Planning Board* (Baltimore: Johns Hopkins University Press, 1981) and Philip W. Warken, *A History of the National Resources Planning Board 1933–1943* (New York: Garland Publishing, 1979).
48. Roosevelt also included "the right to adequate protection from the economic fears of old age, sickness, accident and unemployment." *US Senate, Special Committee on Unemployment Problems, Readings in Unemployment,* 86th Cong., 1st Sess. (Washington, DC: US Government Printing Office, 1960), pp. 1–2.
49. Full Employment Bill of 1945, S. 380, 79th Cong., 1st Sess., reprinted in *Hearing before the Subcommittee on Equal Opportunities of the Committee on Education and Labor, House of Representatives,* 93rd. Cong., 2nd Sess., on H.R. 15476, Oct. 8, 1974, pp. 70–73.
50. Quoted in Russell A. Nixon, "The Historical Development of the Conception and Implementation of Full Employment as Economic Policy," in Alan Gartner, Russell A. Nixon, and Frank Riessman, eds., *Public Service Employment: An Analysis of Its History, Problems, and Prospects* (New York: Praeger, 1973), p. 27. See also Helen Ginsburg, *Full Employment and Public Policy: The United States and Sweden* (Lexington, MA: Lexington Books, 1983), pp. 16–17, in which she cites the Conference Report explaining the difference between the two terms.
51. Nels Anderson, *The Right to Work* (New York: Modern Age Books, 1938), p. 65.

52. Letter from J.C. Lindsey to Perry A. Fellows, Administrative Office, FERA, 10 December 1934, in National Archives, Record Group 69, FERA Series 8: Goods, Production of, for Unemployed.
53. Harry L. Hopkins, *Spending to Save: The Complete Story of Relief* (New York: W. W. Norton, 1936), p. 125.
54. Anderson, *The Right to Work*, p. 92.

Notes on Contributors

Richard B. Dadzie is Assistant Professor of Economics and Finance at the University of Hawaii-West Oahu in Pearl City, Hawaii. He holds a Ph.D. in Economics and Geosciences from the University of Missouri–Kansas City. His research focuses on comparative studies of development between sub-Saharan Africa and South East Asia, and his past work has included collaborations with the Central Regional Development Commission in Cape Coast, Ghana, Ministry of Food and Agriculture, Cape Coast, Ghana, and the Institute of East Asian Studies at the University of Malaysia–Sarawak in Kota Samarahan, Sarawak, Malaysia. Richard has been involved in various research projects on labor issues including a piece on engaging the youth in productive employment in Ghana. He was awarded a Dissertation Research Fellowship and a Preparing Future Faculty Fellowship during his time at the University of Missouri–Kansas City.

Poulomi Dasgupta is in the Department of Economics and Finance at St. Peters College in Jersey City, NJ. She is a Ph.D. candidate in Economics at the University of Missouri–Kansas City. She received a Masters from Mumbai University with specialization in Industrial Economics and Monetary Economics. She has previously been a researcher for *Economic and Political Weekly* in Mumbai and the Center for Full Employment and Price Stability. She is also an alumnus of the African Program on Rethinking Development Economics. Her research areas are Development Economics, Macroeconomics, and Political Economy. Her doctoral research encompasses employment generation programs and their impact on long-term development, political economy of developing countries, impact of colonial rule on developing countries in particular India, and rural economics. She has also conducted field research in India on the National Rural Employment Guarantee Act and its impact on asset creation under the scheme.

Mathew Forstater is Professor of Economics at the University of Missouri–Kansas City, Director of the Center for Full Employment and Price Stability, and Research Associate with the Jerome Levy Economics Institute. He is the author of *Little Book of Big Ideas: Economics*. He is also the author of numerous journal articles, working papers, and policy reports on unemployment, full employment, green jobs, money, and competing approaches to the debt and deficit. He received his Ph.D. from the New School for Social Research.

Antoine Godin is a Ph.D. candidate at the University of Pavia in Italy. He earned a Masters in Engineering from the Université Catholique de Louvain and a Masters in Cooperation and Development Studies from the Instituto Universitario di Studi Superiori di Pavia. Godin earned a three-year scholarship from the Italian government in 2009.

Josefina Y. Li is Instructor of Economics at Bemidji State University. She is a Ph.D. candidate at the University of Missouri–Kansas City and a Research Assistant with the Center for Full Employment and Price Stability where she regularly contributes to The State of Black Kansas City. Previously, Professor Li served on the conference organizing committee for the 10th International Post Keynesian Conference. Her research interests include ecological economics and history of economic thought.

Michael J. Murray is Assistant Professor of Economics at Bemidji State University and a Research Associate with the Center for Full Employment and Price Stability. He received his Ph.D. from the University of Missouri–Kansas City. His current research focuses on simulations of various Employer of Last Resort proposals, heterodox price and production modeling, and the economics of Adolph Lowe. He has published in the *Review of Radical Political Economy*, *Journal of Economic Issues*, served as a book reviewer for the *Heterodox Economics Newsletter*, and contributed to edited volumes.

Nancy E. Rose is Professor Emeritus of Economics at California State University, San Bernardino. She is the author of *Put to Work: The WPA and Public Employment in the Great Depression* (New York: Monthly Review Press, 1994; 2nd ed. 2009) and *Workfare or Fair Work: Women, Welfare, and Government Work Programs* (New Brunswick, NJ: Rutgers University Press, 1995). She has also published numerous articles on social welfare policy, radical pedagogy and lesbian, gay, bisexual parented families in journals such as *Feminist Economics*, *Journal of Economic Issues*, *Feminist Studies*, *Social Service Review*, *the Review of Radical Political Economics*, *the Journal of Progressive Human Services*, *Affilia: Journal of Women and Social Work*, and *the Journal of Sociology and Social Welfare.*

Pavlina R. Tcherneva is Assistant Professor of Economics at Bard College. She has previously taught at Franklin and Marshall College and the University of Missouri–Kansas City. During 2000–2006, Pavlina served as the Associate Director for Economic Analysis at the Center for Full Employment and Price Stability, where she remains a research associate. In Summer 2006, she was a visiting scholar at the University of Cambridge Centre for Economic and Public Policy, UK, and since July 2007, she has been a research scholar at the Levy Economics Institute. Pavlina conducts research in the fields of public policy and monetary theory and has collaborated with policymakers from Argentina, Bulgaria, China, Turkey, and the United States on developing and evaluating various job creation programs. Her articles have appeared in the *Journal of Post Keynesian Economics*, *Journal of Economic Issues*, *International Journal of Political Economy*, *Rutgers Journal of Law and Urban Policy*, *International Journal of Environment, Workplace, and Employment*, and others. She is the coeditor of *Full Employment and Price Stability: The Macroeconomic Vision of William S. Vickrey* (Elgar 2004). Pavlina holds a B.A. in mathematics and economics (Phi Beta Kappa) from Gettysburg College and an M.A. and Ph.D. in economics from the University of Missouri–Kansas City.

Index

The manufacturer's authorised representative in the EU is Springer Nature Customer Service Centre GmbH, Europaplatz 3, 69115 Heidelberg, Germany. If you have any concerns regarding our products, please contact ProductSafety@springernature.com

Printed and bound by CPI Group (UK) Ltd, Croydon, CR0 4YY
14/10/2026
02233132-0003